EMOTIONS
An Owner's Manual

Harness the power of your
greatest personal resource
for life and work

Joie Seldon

outskirts
press

To my husband Bob, whose love, honesty and partnership made writing this book possible.

Table of Contents

Preface

When I began teaching about emotions in 1999, there were not many books out there about Emotional Intelligence. While Daniel Goleman did not invent Emotional Intelligence, nor coin the phrase (Peter Salovey did) his 1995 book **Emotional Intelligence** brought the term and concept to a wide audience.

Now, there are hundreds of books on Emotional Intelligence. This is actually good news. Many have great information. However, what is often missing is an in-depth explanation of what emotions themselves actually *are*.

This book is a contribution to this incredibly important topic from a unique point of view. It is about the universal language that every human being shares. It focuses on the overall function and purpose of emotions, and four cornerstone emotions that are the foundation for all feelings.

My passion for understanding emotions began over forty years ago with a sudden realization that I did not have to accept the misery I was experiencing then as my fate. At that time, I vowed to find out what the truth was about life. I wanted to understand not only myself but also humanity as a whole.

My quest for this "truth" lead to many years of self-realization work, self-guided study, formal education, and years of experience working with clients, all of which led me to this conclusion: There is no ultimate, all-encompassing truth. There is only the moment-to-moment truth of how we feel about what is happening, and we are guided to this truth by our emotions.

When you understand and speak the universal language of emotions, you will be able to converse with anyone through both words and actions in a manner that brings about optimal results for both you and those you are interacting with. Using these skills, you will be able to speak and live your truth in a manner that is respectful to others and without self-sacrifice.

ONE

Welcome and Overview

Welcome to the sometimes daunting, yet thoroughly fascinating world of emotions. Since at least the Middle Ages, we've been living in a world that has devalued emotions. So many emotions are labeled as "negative" that it can be hard to realize the profound value all emotions hold. Yet being in touch with the full range of your emotions can not only be informative and empowering, it also makes for a richer life.

We all have beliefs and attitudes about emotions that come from our family and the culture in which we live. **This Emotional Inheritance influences your response to every situation**. Ingrained responses can easily have unintended consequences. The results can be so profound as to prevent you from being the master of your own fate.

The aim of this owner's manual is to empower you to utilize your emotions as the invaluable resource they are meant to be. I will be providing practical information that offers a unique perspective, useful exercises to help you integrate your experience, and easy-to-apply skills that will increase your Emotional Intelligence and improve your ability to express yourself in positive and productive ways.

While you will learn how to access, understand and express your emotions, this work goes beyond technique. It is about you coming home to yourself, to be wholly who you are, and to be the best of who you are meant to be, so you can live a healthier, more successful, and more fulfilling life.

Students of this work report greater self-confidence and self-trust, less stress, better communication skills, healthier relationships, the release of long-held emotional pain, and the ability to take action on those things that matter to them most.

I'd like to ask you a question. **What are emotions?** What exactly are we talking about here? I've asked this question many times over the years, and it is clear to me that the majority of people have never thought about this question, let alone the answer.

Here is my definition:

Emotions are a physiological, meaning body-based, information system, the purpose of which is to bring you knowledge that prompts you to action that is optimally beneficial for your survival and well-being.

I will elaborate on this in just a moment.

To keep this topic manageable we will focus on four primary emotions that I refer to as the *cornerstone emotions*. They create a foundation from which you will have a greater understanding and mastery of all other feelings. These emotions are fear, anger, sadness, and joy.

Primary emotions are the ones we are biologically hard-wired for. I hold that there are seven primary emotions, and I offer a downloadable article on my website where I briefly discuss the other three, which are shame, disgust, and passion.

You will learn the core information carried in each of the cornerstone emotions, how their purpose has evolved to serve a socially complex world, and how they impact your life when they are not handled well, among other things.

In order for you to get the most out of this material, I am now going to outline four principles that will give you a context for the material presented, and how to apply it to your daily life. Here we go.

Laying the Groundwork - The Four Principles

1. Emotions are an Information System
2. Emotions are Biological
3. Emotions are Inherently Positive
4. Emotions are Energy in Motion

Principle #1 - Emotions are an Information System

First and foremost, emotions are a body-based system; in the same way you have a skeletal system, a nervous system, a vascular system. The function of this system is to bring you information about your relationship to everything. Whether it is what is outside of you – your relationship with people, events, circumstances, worldviews, and more; or what is inside of you – your relationship with yourself, your self-image, memories, and, most significantly, your beliefs.

The purpose of this *emotion system* is to help you to survive, thrive and navigate through life. Each primary emotion has an inherent message that moves you away from pain and harm, or towards vitality and pleasure.

Emotions operate on three levels – primal, primary, and feelings.

Primitive humans started out with **primal** or **instinctual emotions**, akin to our animal friends. These emotions are all about survival. When the caveman or cavewoman encountered a saber tooth tiger they did not stop and think, "What should I do?" The fight-or-flight response kicked in without conscious thought, where fear made them run, or anger made them fight.

We still have these instinctual emotions. And, as we have evolved into a far more complex society, our emotions have also evolved.

The second level is comprised of **primary emotions**, which we can think of as *matured primal emotions*. We are hardwired for these emotions. The focus of this manual is to help you understand both the complexity of how these primary emotions impact us and at the same time know the basic and easy-to-understand meaning they convey.

Finally, there are **feelings**, which are a combination of primary emotions and thoughts. This is where the nuance of emotions comes into play, where you can experience a wide variety of feelings.

In order to function fully, we need all three levels: the primal level for those unfortunate situations where our life might be threatened and we need to act faster than we can think; primary emotions, which are at the core of all emotional experiences, and the myriad of feelings that express the complexity of who we are and our social interactions.

Principle #2 - Emotions are Biological

Emotions are biological, and therefore physiological. You know you are experiencing an emotion because you feel it in your body. That does not mean your thoughts do not affect emotions, or your emotions do not affect thoughts. They do. However, emotions are *never* just "all in your head."

Thanks to innovative psychologists who recognized that the body, not just the mind, is where we experience our emotional and psychological beingness, and to neuroscience and modern technology, we now know a lot about the brain and body functions of emotions. If you want to read more on this, there is a bibliography of recommended books and articles at the end of this manual.

In the sections on each emotion, I will be going over specifics about what goes on in your body and the commonly felt sensations that you experience as they pertain to that particular emotion.

For now, it is important to understand that emotions are experienced in the body and that they have a profound purpose. To benefit from the gift of your emotions, it is necessary to actually *feel* them. It is important to allow yourself the visceral experience of your emotions. It will help you to stop judging yourself, and others, for having certain emotions that you have been taught are bad or wrong.

Our resistance to feeling our emotions often comes because we feel uncomfortable in our body and we do whatever it takes to feel "better." Much of commercial advertising is based on selling you things that are supposed to make you feel good (as if feeling uncomfortable, for even a moment, is bad; as if somehow you have failed).

Instead of trying to stop the uncomfortable sensation of an emotion through denial, repression or avoidant behavior, you can utilize the felt sensations in your body to help you recognize exactly what emotion you are feeling. Once you know what you are feeling, you will be able to comprehend its inherent message. I will get into more detail about that later in this manual.

It is feeling an emotion with awareness that gives you the power to make a conscious choice as to what you are going to do with that feeling. **The more aware you are of your emotions, the more power you have to be in charge of your life.**

Most self-limiting behavior and addictions, large and small, stem from attempts to avoid feeling certain emotions you believe will be too painful, or that you judge yourself as bad or wrong for having. Yet being willing to go through the experience of feeling your body sensations can free you. I cannot tell you how many times clients of mine, after finally allowing themselves to feel the emotions they had been resisting, sometimes for years, have said to me, "It wasn't nearly as bad as I thought it would be! What was I so afraid of?"

With that realization, they learned that experiencing their emotions actually *reduced* their pain. And, it freed up the energy they were using to suppress what was true for them.

The habit of avoiding emotions is understandable. We all have habits of behavior that help us to maintain order in our life. These automatic responses begin in childhood as survival strategies and develop over time. As we get older, we mature and grow in consciousness, but often, old habits remain.

This is because these habits are literally ingrained in your body. Your brain has laid down neuronal pathways that prompt predictable behavior so you don't have to reinvent yourself every morning when you wake up. These patterns are also in your body's cellular memory, your muscles, and nervous system. All supported by subconscious beliefs.

Have you ever had the experience where you say or do something and later think, "Oh my God, I can't believe I said/did that! What is wrong with me? That's not who I am." You judge yourself for behaving in old ways. You feel stuck. You want to change, but you do not know how.

The key to changing unwanted patterns in yourself, understanding the behavior of others, and making your life work a lot better lies in your willingness to feel your emotions.

The foundation of emotional intelligence is self-awareness. You must be self-aware before you can fully glean the benefits your emotions. And you cannot be self-aware without feeling emotions in your body.

Principle #3 - Emotions are Positive

Because emotions are part of our biological functioning and because we need them for our survival, all primary emotions (emotions in their purest form) must be positive. By positive, I mean they are constructive in nature.

When you label an emotion as negative, it can make you not want to feel it. What limits us is judging the emotions we are having. The problem is not with the emotion itself, but how we repress it, stuff it, deny it, or become overwhelmed by it.

All primary emotions are positive. Just as joy is a positive emotion, so are sadness, fear, and anger.

Principle #4 - Emotions are Energy in Motion

The Latin root of emotions is the word emovere, which means to move out. Emotions are meant to bring you the information you need, and then move out.

The energy of each emotion has a particular kind of vibration and a direction of movement. I will talk more about this in the sections on each the four specific emotions.

The Problems of Mismanaged Emotions

There are two key problem areas related to emotional mismanagement: physical health and interpersonal relationships.

First, because emotions are biological, the energy of unprocessed emotions stays in your body until it is dealt with. Clearly, not all disease is emotion based. However, there is a myriad of health issues that can stem from unprocessed emotions, which in turn can trigger a depleted immune system, ongoing muscle tension, excessive stress, and more. Depression, ulcers, intestinal disorders, fatigue, heart disease, back problems; the list of ailments that can be related to unprocessed emotions is endless.

In 1994 I had a sizable melanoma tumor removed from my leg. After careful research, and soul-search, I chose diet, alternative healing, and emotional processing as my healing tactic. I discovered long-held grief and anger towards my father that I had not been conscious of. Not only did I survive, I grew closer to my father. Which leads me to the second key.

The other big problem area is in our relationships, personal and professional. Nothing impacts a relationship more than unexpressed, or inappropriately expressed emotions. The biggest relationship issues stem from the inability to communicate feelings in productive ways.

More about relationships will be addressed in the sections on each emotion.

How to Use this Manual

There are four sections, one on each of the cornerstone emotions. Each section has a segment on the inherent meaning and function of that emotion, followed by exercises that help you 1) develop body awareness of your own emotional experience, 2) release unprocessed emotions from your past, and 3) teach you skills to manage that emotion in present time.

There is a variety of exercises and processes from which to choose to suit your unique needs and way of learning. It is not necessary to do them all. This manual is meant as a resource that you can return to time and again as a reference when you need help with a specific area.

Something important to keep in mind is that this information is not just about technique and intellectual understanding. It is about experience. Sometimes just reading a section may evoke certain experiences, and digesting it in your own time can effect positive change. Other times, it can be extremely beneficial to do an exercise in order to fully comprehend the information.

While you may not always be comfortable feeling your emotions, this work need not be heavy or overly serious. The intent is to help you feel better. This work can be enjoyable and satisfying. It can actually be fun to feel the full range of emotions!

That said, you may feel exhausted after doing an exercise because you have released a lot of energy that has been held over time. More often than not, you will feel energized and enlivened.

If you choose to go directly to a specific emotion, I invite you to, at some point in time, come back to the beginning and work through the rest. When you come to the emotion you have already worked with, review the material and make note of what you have learned, how your relationship to that emotion has changed, or not, and how you can continue to grow in your understanding and expression of that emotion.

TWO

The Necessity of Fear

The Dichotomy of Fear

Fear is dichotomous. It can save your life, or it can really mess it up. It can compel you in an instant to action that moves you out of harm's way. Or, it can lurk insidiously just beneath consciousness, stopping you from taking action on your dreams and goals, keeping you from saying what you really want to say, stifling your creativity, and undermining belief in yourself.

In this segment, you will learn how to be in charge of your fear, rather than it being in charge of you, and how to benefit from its message. I want to start by talking about two distinct functions of fear.

One is the **primal function** of fear, which is to protect you from death or bodily harm. In life-threatening situations, fear's message is "DANGER!" It is one-half of the *fight-or-flight response*. Its job is to move you to action faster than you can consciously decide. You need fear. Your life depends on it.

The other is the **primary function** of fear, or what I call ego-based fear, which has evolved out of fear's primal purpose of survival in order to serve the complex interactions of human beings. Now, by ego-based, I do not mean self-centeredness or arrogance. Rather it refers to our Self Identity, which is a combination of our conscious and unconscious sense of Self. *This* fear has to do with our relationship to others, to circumstance, and to the world at large.

Most of us experience fear not because our life is being threatened, but rather because we are threatened with change, rejection, or being hurt emotionally. Nothing sends a shiver of fear up your spine like those four little words, "We need to talk."

We also have a **fear of the unknown**. Why do people stay in unhappy and unsatisfying relationships or jobs that bore them? Often it is fear of the unknown. There is predictability in the status quo. Even when we don't like the status quo, it is familiar; we know what to do with it, we have a strategy in place. One reason change can be difficult is because it often involves the unknown.

When we experience a threat to our emotional self, the fear alert goes off. But its message is not there *is* danger, rather it is "PAY ATTENTION, there *might* be danger." It is about *potential* threat.

The difference in these two experiences, direct physical threat and potential emotional threat, where they overlap, and how to manage them, is the focus of this chapter on fear.

Three Keys to Managing Fear

1. The first is to understand the physical aspects of the primal fear response, what is actually happening in your body.
2. The second is how and why this fear response manifests in daily life.
3. The third is how ego-based fear also protects us, and how to manage that kind of fear so it does not become debilitating.

Key #1: The Physiology of Fear

The fundamental purpose of fear is self-preservation. Fear compels the body to act in service of its own survival. It is a biological response to threat, best known as part of the fight-or-flight response. Because fear's very function is to get you to act faster than you can think, when your life is threatened it takes over and there really is nothing to manage.

It is important to understand this primary function in order to put your daily fear responses in a context that will help you manage the more subtle aspects of fear, the one's that have a negative impact on your life.

We start by looking at the primal fear response. Have you ever been driving a car and had a narrow miss, where you swerved out of the way of another car or slammed on your breaks without thinking? In those situations, your body has taken control.

In the fraction of a second it takes to avoid getting hit by another car, alert signals flash in your brain before you are fully conscious of what is happening. Adrenaline and other hormones flood your system sending messages from the seat of your emotional brain, the amygdala, through the central nervous system to parts of your body. Your heart beats faster pumping extra blood to your arm and leg muscles giving you the energy and strength to move instantly.

We see this automatic response in stories of heroes who say, "I'm no hero, I didn't think about what I was doing, I just did it."

When in fear, nonessential functions slow down or stop in order to concentrate resources on your survival. That is why some people pee or defecate when extremely frightened. Vocal cords contract causing a person to scream or yell. A milder version of this is when someone's voice goes up in pitch when they are nervous.

All of this is regulated by the Autonomic Nervous System or ANS. The ANS is a key player in the realm of emotions. It regulates all of your automatic body functions like breathing, heartbeat, and digestion. The ANS has two parts that work in congruence with each other called the Sympathetic and the Parasympathetic branches. When you feel fear it is the Sympathetic part that gets activated.

When blood rushes to your muscles, blood flow is diminished in your brain. At the same time, brain activity gives priority to messages from the emotional brain and limits messages from the rational thinking part of the brain, the frontal cortex. In extreme cases, you literally cannot think.

When your body responds in this way, once you act and the dangerous situation is resolved, the second part of the ANS, the Parasympathetic Nervous System, takes over. It stops the secretion of stress hormones, slows your heart rate down and allows you to breathe deeper, calming you down. Depending on the level of danger, it can take a while for you to actually feel calm because you need to eliminate the stress charge and hormones from your body.

There is one more piece to this. In order for the body to react that quickly, the neurological mechanism of fear in your brain does not recognize specifics. It recognizes *possibilities*. Something only has to *resemble* a threat for the fear system to kick in. Neuroscientist Joseph LeDoux, in his book "The Emotional Brain," says that failing to respond to danger is more costly than responding inappropriately to a benign stimulus. In other words, it is better to *overreact* to a non-threat than to *not react strongly enough* to a real threat. So, we err on the side of overreacting.

> *You are walking in the woods and out of the corner of your eye you see something that makes you jump and let out a shriek, only to realize it's not a snake, but a stick that looks like a snake. You take a deep breath, shutter a little and may even let out a sigh, or little laugh. This shutter, breath, and sigh is your Parasympathetic Nervous System at work, calming you down.*

Bottom line, your Autonomic Nervous System causes you to respond to potential threat instantly and automatically. The problems arise when you experience aspects of this primal fear response in non-life threatening situations.

To reiterate, **the first key to managing fear is to understand the physiology of it**. In order to survive in life, you must have ready access to the ability to act faster than you can think. Next, we will see how this primal fear mechanism operates in your daily life.

Before moving on to key #2, try to remember a time when you had this sudden rush of fear that caused you to react, whether or not there was an actual threat, such as a near freeway miss or airplane turbulence. Notice if anything happens in your body just thinking about it.

Key #2: How the Primal Instinct Operates in Your Daily Life

The second key to managing fear is to know how the primal instinct operates in your modern daily life. There are two points to understand here.

First, the fight-or-flight instinct has four components. Unless your life is directly threatened, the sequence is actually *freeze, fight, flight, faint*. The purpose of *freeze* is to give you time to assess the situation. It is the "stop and pay attention" part of the ego fear response.

We can easily see this behavior in animals.

I often hike in an area where I encounter deer. If they don't bolt immediately, they look at me and freeze. I can see their nose twitching to smell me, eyes staring, ears turned towards me listening. All of their senses are focused on determining whether or not I am a threat. When they sense I am not a threat, they swish their tail, shimmy a little as they exhale, and turn back to their grazing. You may have witnessed similar behavior in dogs or other animals. They shimmy to shake off the electromagnetic charge that occurs when the sympathetic nervous system is activated. Animals do what they need to do instinctively.

We also use our senses. During the *freeze* state, our energy is concentrated in the upper body and around our head, the locus of our sense of sight, smell, hearing, and taste. Our upper body is contracted and we barely breathe, so that we too can be still enough to assess if there is a threat.

Unlike animals, we humans have lost our instinct to shake off the freeze. It is easy to get stuck there, leading to a constant and often unconscious state of tension and shallow breathing, which by the way limits the amount of oxygen going to your brain.

If you are already carrying tension from the daily stresses of life, a non-life-threatening fear response can be particularly subtle and hard to recognize as a fear you need to process.

A word about the *faint* part of *freeze fight, flight, faint*. In the wild, some animals will only eat animals they kill themselves. So a primal instinct for their prey is to literally faint. The predator assumes its prey is dead so it moves on. In humans, what this looks like is going numb or disassociating. Your mind goes blank or goes to totally unrelated thoughts. In essence, you check out.

Take a moment now and tune into your body. Simply notice what tension, if any, you are feeling. Where do you feel it most? Notice your breathing. Where does your breath stop? How long have you had that tension? Is it chronic or recent? Notice what it is like to feel that tension consciously.

Now, take a deep breath, deep enough to move your diaphragm. As you exhale relax your muscles. See if you can let go of the tension. Do that again. Inhale . . . exhale . . . and let go. One more time, inhale . . . exhale . . . and relax. Notice if it is easy to let go, or not. If you do relax, notice what that feels like.

——————— • ♦ • ———————

I want to offer an example of an experience of getting stuck in the *freeze* state. Have you ever had a strong reaction to something, but stopped yourself from saying or doing what you really wanted to say or do because you are afraid of the consequences? Then afterward, you ruminate on the situation by enacting in your imagination what you wish you had said or done. You cannot seem to stop thinking about it, repeating what you wish you had said over and over.

That is you getting stuck in the *freeze* part of the fear response. Your rumination is an attempt to take action to release the charge that is still in your body. But this kind internal obsessing is not a productive action.

In a situation like this, in order to release that charge, you have to either find a way to take an effective action or communicate what you want to say, hopefully appropriately, or you have to release that charge from your body.

There are a number of ways to do this, journaling or talking it out with a friend or therapist, even some kind of physical activity can help, *if* you set an intention to release the energy. Venting in a way that keeps you stirred up with self-righteous indignation never helps. I will be offering exercises in the next chapter for releasing fear.

How Past Experiences Impact the Present

Remember, your primal fear response mobilizes in the Amygdala, which is also where memories of things you experienced as harmful or threatening are stored.

Your body is always ready to protect itself, and it is particularly responsive to anything that resembles a fearful or painful experience from the past. Our survival instinct to keep from repeating past experiences that hurt us is a large part of ego-based fear.

It is also important to know that the memories that get activated are often unconscious. They have been forgotten, repressed, or they stem from a pre-verbal experience that happened before you could talk, so you do not have an intellectual awareness of it. This adds to a sense of vulnerability when we are afraid. Not only is there a potential threat from the future, there is an unconscious threat coming from your past.

The impact of past experiences set up patterns of behavior that do not serve you in present time. When you are young you are simply trying to make sense of what is happening to you. So, you develop beliefs that explain things. This does not mean these beliefs are true.

The combination of unconscious painful memories being triggered, along with getting stuck in the freeze stage of the fear response makes it harder to come back to a state of equilibrium.

The most important thing you can do to keep from getting stuck in fear is to stay consciously present with it as you feel the sensations of fear in present time.

———————◆•———————

Early in my marriage, a wise person recommended my husband and I have Talk Time once a week in order to have a designated, neutral space to communicate.

In the beginning, I was always really nervous at the start of these talks. As a child, I had been told many times "children should be seen and not heard." When I did speak up, I felt judged. Even though honest communication was extremely important to me, and a top priority in my marriage, I was afraid to express myself honestly to my husband.

Sometimes he would start by saying, "This is really hard to say." My body would freeze. Heart pounding, palms sweating, I'd sit there barely breathing as my husband struggled to express him-self. If I was the one who had something hard to say, I felt the same kind of terror.

I wasn't thinking at all about my family history at that point, but I knew the intensity of my fear was extreme. It was by staying present with that fear that I was able to recognize it as my sub-conscious mind's anticipation of rejection from someone who loved me.

My body was saying, "PAY ATTENTION! This could be danger-ous." Yet by being present with my fear, I was able to stay open to what my husband was saying, and work through the delicate stages of developing trust. I learned a lot about my own insecuri-ties during those talks. I also learned to express my true feelings and to hear those of my husband. Sometimes it was really hard to do but so worth the discomfort and awkwardness. It's been twenty-two years since we had those talks, and we have a rock solid relationship.

If I had allowed my fear to dictate my behavior, I know we would have ended up in a power struggle. Instead, we grew closer, we trusted each other more, and developed a collabora-tive relationship.

———— ◆ ————

Before moving on to the 3rd Key to managing fear in your daily life, you may want to take a moment now to notice what comes to mind related to what you have read so far?

Is there some action or communication you have been unable to take? Is there a person you always feel tense around? Are there cer-tain situations where you tend to freeze up? As you think about these, notice what happens in your body. Take some time to recognize how fear may be operating on an unconscious level in your life. You may want to take some notes on things to work with later in the exercise segment.

Key #3: Ego-Based Fear Also Protects You

The third key to managing fear is to understand how ego-based fear also protects you, and how to cope with this kind of fear so it does not become debilitating. This will help you to be in charge of your choices, and respond more consciously to stimulus rather than react automatically to it.

To briefly recap, we have a primal fear system that responds to potential threat faster than we can think in order for the body to survive. And we have an ego-based fear system whose message is "Stop and Pay attention, there *might* be a threat, but not necessarily." This is often experienced as a kind of freeze, or stillness, so you have time to assess whether or not there is a threat. And, it is possible to get stuck in the tension of the freeze stage.

Now, when our fear response is not due to a direct attack, it is a response to potential, anticipated, or imagined threat. The problem with this is that we so easily anticipate or imagine the worst-case scenario! Your significant other says, "We need to talk," and in the span of a few seconds, your mind races to the future where the relationships is over – *"How am I going to deal with breaking up, what's life is going to be like on my own, what about the dog, the apartment, the CD collection . . . oh my God!"*

You lose your job. While it is totally understandable for you to feel fear, there is a difference between thinking, *"OK, I'm scared, but I need to deal with this. What are my options?"* and a feeling of panic and chaos, or a sense of doom that leads you to think *"Oh my God! I'm going to lose my savings, my car, my house!"*

In these scenarios, what commonly happens is the rest of the world drops away and you are totally focused on your crisis and the impending consequences. That is understandable.

But, when you succumb to *worst-case scenario* thinking, you are no longer in the present, but projecting out into the future. Yes, it is possible that these things *could* happen, but reacting as if they *will* happen keeps you in a state of tension and narrows your scope of thinking.

This kind of projecting is not limited to a major crisis. At the beginning of a recent coaching call, my client was in such an aggravated state that she said it felt like having a panic attack. Professionally, she handles complex high-stakes negotiations on a daily basis. What triggered her extreme state of anxiety that day were a couple of small glitches that had no consequences to the deal she was working on. With some coaching, she was able to calm her nervous system and understand why her reaction was so extreme. She was actually letting off steam that had built up over the week. She could afford to on the small things precisely because there was nothing at stake. Once she became calm, solutions to those glitches came to her in an instant.

Because she took the time to process what happened, she came to understand how important it is for her to manage her stress level every day. Letting tension build up over time did not benefit her professionally, or personally.

Projecting worst-case scenarios limit your ability to access resources that will help you make the best choices so those things *won't* happen.

Fear of the Unknown

The hardest fear to manage is the **fear of the unknown.** Everyone experiences this fear. It is part of life. It is what you do with it that makes the difference. There are two common ways we cope with fear of the unknown that do not serve us.

First, fear of the unknown can make you overly controlling, trying to guarantee outcomes. This shows up in a number of ways:

- Being a perfectionist and placing high demands on yourself and others.
- Micromanaging employees, your children, or your spouse.
- Being chronically critical or threatening.

———————◆———————

When I was thirty-five I went to visit my parents in Austin, Texas.

I planned to go hear a friend of mine's band play at a club on Austin's famous 6th Street, where the South by Southwest Festival got started. In spite of the fact that I had been living on my own since I was eighteen, half of my life, my mother got so upset that I would go to "dangerous" 6th Street by myself, that she actually threatened to kill herself if I went. Her threat was a way of controlling her fear by controlling me. While I knew she would not actually do herself in, it is a pretty lousy thing to hear from your own mother.

It is no wonder I grew up a perfectionist! For me, I learned how to let go of controlling behavior in my marriage. My husband is the sweetest person in the world, but he would not put up with any domineering behavior from me; for which I am sincerely grateful.

———— ◆ ————

You may take the opposite tact by letting life lead you, rather than taking charge of where you are going. Like a client I will call Jack, who was an account manager in a big company. He had a degree in finance because that is what his parents wanted. For twenty-five years he had taken stable jobs, made safe choices, and gone along with what others wanted. When the company he worked for downsized, he was given notice. He felt that if he did not make a change now, her never would. And, he was terrified.

Once he began to fully *feel* his fear, several core limiting beliefs became evident. Chief among them was that he was not worthy of doing something for a living that he loved. 'Think of others, and never of your self' was his family's motto. He was able to dismantle this limiting belief by first feeling the impact of it consciously. He then took action by enrolling in several classes in the field he had always wanted to work in.

Do you have a fear of the unknown? One that keeps you from doing something you really want to do?

When you have unacknowledged fear, it becomes a lens through which you interpret everything that happens to you. It can deeply limit your ability to take action on what you desire or to connect with and be authentic with others.

Fear of Who We Are

It is easy to view fear as being a defense against outside forces. However, sometimes what you actually fear is inside. You fear your own inadequacies.

This can be particularly difficult. None of us wants to face the negative beliefs we have about our self. The most debilitating are the ones that say, *"There must be something wrong with me. I am a flawed being."* or *"I'm unlovable."* Where we feel separate from others in an irreparable way.

Besides fear, this kind of belief prompts a feeling of toxic shame. Because these two are so linked together, I want to say a quick word about shame. There are two kinds of shame, one is healthy, and one is toxic. Healthy shame is a primary emotion and its message is one of remorse. I have done something I feel bad about, and I own up to it. It is your internal moral compass that tells you when you have crossed a line. As Tom Bradshaw says in his book "Healing the Shame That Binds You," shame lets you know you are not perfect.

Toxic shame is not a primary emotion. This is an important distinction. It is a feeling born out of fear and a belief that something is fundamentally wrong with you. Toxic shame is always put on you by something outside of you, other people's words, or their treatment of you.

Tom struggled with this issue for years. He used perfectionism as a way to overcome his flaws. If he could just do something perfectly it would prove he was not so awful after all. He was often angry at work because no one, least of all himself, could live up to his standards. It took getting fired from a job he loved to make him seek help.

What makes the belief that you are fundamentally flawed so painful is that it means you are separate from the rest of humanity. Bottom line, separation from others and abject loneliness are what we fear most of all. So much of what stops us from being emotionally honest with others is the fear of being judged or rejected.

The highest value of being emotionally honest with yourself, even when the emotions are hard to experience, is that it always points to deeper truths. Tom had to start with feeling his fear and toxic shame consciously before he could move beyond it and recognize the lie that he was fundamentally flawed, the one he had come to believe.

As the saying goes, "the truth shall set you free." When you can access those internal fears that point to your beliefs, you then have something very specific to work with.

The Habit of Fear

Now, some good news. Your fear responses are often just habits. A lot of times it is not that big a deal to make a change. Simply noticing subtle freezes, hesitations, or anxieties that happen in your daily life and breathing your way through it can help you shift. By putting your attention in the here and now and being curious, you may find it is a simple matter of a fear of the unknown you are experiencing. Then you can recognize that the best antidote to that fear is to be present in the moment and make conscious choices.

It may take some time to dismantle the old habit and develop new ones, but it is absolutely doable.

The Relationship Between Fear and Stress

I want to close this segment on fear by saying a word about stress. Whatever the source of your stress, if it goes on too long without breaks that restore you, it will impair your ability to think clearly and play havoc with your health.

This is not news. Yet it is easy to get caught up in the urgency of the moment and not take the steps you need to take care of yourself. Stress weakens your immune system, interrupts your sleep, taxes your heart and produces chronic muscle tension. Tranquilizers, antidepressants, and anti-anxiety medications account for one-fourth of all prescriptions written in the U.S.

You do not need to eliminate stress altogether; some stress is actually good for you. It can push you to step up to a challenge and show you what you are made of. What can benefit you most is to learn how to respond to situations that diminish the amount of stress you experience. The information and tools in this manual can help you not only handle the stress you have, but actually lessen the amount of stress you experience by preventing it.

I am going to name some common symptoms that may indicate you have unprocessed fear. As you read each one, I invite you to sense if you have fears you are not fully aware of.

These symptoms are:

- Procrastination. What are you putting off because of fear?

- Making excuses for why you are not doing something you say you want to do.

- Lack of relationships and/or lack of intimacy in your relationships. You may have many different feelings about this; just focus on fear for now.

- Feeling isolated or lonely.

- Feeling stuck.

Any fears that you uncover can be processed in the exercises that follow this chapter. Here is a brief recap of the three keys to understanding and managing fear:

- First, primal fear is a biological response to a threat of life and limb that gets you to respond faster than you can think. Its message is Danger!

- Second, there is a way fear shows up in your daily life, what I call ego-based fear. Its message is, "Pay attention. There may be a threat, but not necessarily." This fear is often subtle and can cause problems if not understood and dealt with.

- Third, this ego-based fear also protects us, and there are ways to manage it so it does not become debilitating.

In the next and final segment on fear, there are exercises to:

- help you be more present with the physical sensation of fear,
- provide tools and processes for healthy management of your fear, where you can learn to feel your fear and use it to bring consciousness to what is going on in your world and the choices you make,
- and ways to release old fears that keep you stuck.

THREE

Exercises and Guides for Managing Fear

Overview

I want to give you a quick overview of the exercises first, and then each exercise will be in a separate chapter so you can go directly to it in the future.

First is a foundational exercise where you are going to play a bit and get in touch with the physical manifestation of fear. Sounds like fun, doesn't it?

Then I will share some techniques for managing fear in present time that focus on the body and thought awareness. Finally, there is an exercise to evoke hidden or suppressed fears, and a process to release those.

Once you have gone through an exercise, feel free to adapt or combine them in any way that you want. I invite you to tune into your intuition and sense what might be right for you.

Body awareness is key to managing any of your emotions. Learning to recognize your body's particular sensations makes it possible for you to catch more subtle experiences of fear as well as managing more extreme experiences.

A simple way of understanding the physiology of emotions is to evoke an emotion by thinking of things that make you feel it, something that is fairly easy to do when it comes to emotions like sadness or anger. However, that is not the case with fear. Because fear is activated on such a primal level, it can be hard to feel it when not directly provoked.

Also, your *internal* fears can manifest in *very* subtle ways, where they are often experienced more as tension, stress, or stuckness. By stuckness, I mean when you are having a hard time making a decision or taking action.

As you move through the exercises, keep this in mind, and look for subtle signs such as slight tensions. Key areas to notice are neck and shoulder tension, shallow breathing, solar plexus tension, an increase in heart rate, and stomach or intestinal discomfort.

FOUR

Foundational Exercises — Getting Used to Feeling Fear in Your Body

Exercise 1: Child's Play "Acting As If"

Without having to evoke a genuine experience of fear, acting as if you are afraid can help you develop your capacity to recognize it when it does happen. In a sense, it wakes up your emotional body and gives it the message that *it's OK to feel this.*

I will now guide you through a two-minute exercise. I recommend doing this alone, or with someone who will do it with you. You may feel silly, and that is OK. What you are about to do is an exaggerated version of how fear shows up in your body.

———•◆———

Do the following:

- Bring all your attention to your head and upper body. Tense your neck, your shoulders, upper arms, and upper back muscles. Breathe shallowly. Widen your eyes. Tense your solar plexus. Notice what your hands are doing, and let them do it. If you are doing this with someone, notice how each other looks.

- What does this feel like?

- Where is your focus?

- Now say, or think: "I'm scared! I'm scared! I'm afraid! I'm afraid!"

- Now reduce the tension level by about half, where you are not nearly as tense, but not completely relaxed. (This is a rough approximation of bodily sensations when you experience fear in your daily life.)

- Now, let it go, shake it loose, and breathe normally.

Notice how you feel now. What are you aware of? Use this experience to help you discern when you might be feeling fear, rather than just thinking you are stressed.

Exercise 2: Waking Up to Daily Fears

Remember, Emotional Intelligence starts with self-awareness. This is an observation exercise to help you pay more attention to fears you experience throughout the day. Some things we attribute to stress, such as irritability, headaches, back pain or exhaustion, may actually be unconscious fear.

———— ♦ ————

Kim is a mature woman who is self-employed. She could not afford marketing help so she was doing her own newsletters and social media. A highly capable person, she was often irritable and easily overwhelmed when she went online to promote her business. If she ran into a technical challenge, she would get so upset she would "lose it." One day she sat with her feelings until she realized that under the anger was fear. In a world where others seemed to use social media with ease, she was afraid she would be left behind. Once she got to the truth, her fear went away. She then made some adjustments to the way she promotes her business that was much easier for her.

———— ♦ ————

Pick a day when you will pay attention to your fear response. Set some kind of reminder to go off every couple of hours, like an alert on your computer or cell phone. This will be your reminder to check in with yourself. You are simply going to **pay attention to what you are feeling**.

A good time would be when you know you are going face a new situation, or have an interaction that makes you uncomfortable, like having a challenging conversation with someone. You can even think of something in your career or personal life that you want to do but have been putting off, and commit to doing it. It does not have to be monumental. It could be making a phone call or balancing your checkbook. Put it into your schedule and do it.

If you picked a specific task or situation, be sure to notice what happens in your body when you put it in your schedule, as you think about it, and as you get ready to do it.

Whenever you choose to do your observation, do the following:

1. **Notice sensations**: What is going on in your body? Do you feel any tension and if so where? What is the quality of it? Are you bracing yourself? Do you feel contracted? Are you numb, jittery, ungrounded?

2. **Notice your breathing**. Breath is one of the easiest things to track. In the *freeze* stage of fear, you are holding still and your breath will be shallow. When a client is talking about something that scares them I will ask them to notice their breath and often they will say, "I'm not breathing." They are literally holding their breath.

3. **Notice your thoughts**. Where are you mentally - in the present, or thinking about the past or the future? Are you worrying about something specific, or is your mind muddled or confused? Is there something you are anticipating or ruminating on? If you can, write down your thoughts. If you keep track of the inner dialog, you will find patterns, repetitions. You can learn a lot

about the core message you are giving yourself, which comes from your beliefs.

You may want to put a post-it in a visible place that says: Body - Breath - Thoughts.

I recommend repeating this exercise in different settings or situations, for example at work, at home, or in a social setting. I ask that you simply stay present with your fear for at least a few hours before moving on to the fear management techniques that follow. It is important that you send a message to your subconscious that you are willing to feel your fear and to listen to its message.

Once you are more aware of the physical sensation of your fear, now what do you do?

FIVE

Befriending Your Fear

Saying Yes To Your Fear

The first step in managing your fear is to **acknowledge it**. When you notice a bodily sensation of tension or a thought that makes you anxious, instead of trying to get rid of the feeling, turn your attention toward it. Stay present with your physical sensations and tell yourself the truth, "This is fear." Pay attention to your thoughts, and acknowledge that your thoughts are making you tense. In essence, you are saying yes to what is actually happening.

Being emotionally truthful with yourself enables you to do something positive with what you are feeling. Very often, the simple act of acknowledging a sensation allows your body to relax, at least a little because it is getting what it wants, which is for you to pay attention.

Then, take on an **attitude of curiosity**. Become a curious observer of what is going on inside of you. When you step outside of your experience and become a witness to it, you create space between you and the fear. You no longer identify *as* the fear. Instead, the fear is seen as just one piece of what is happening in your life at that moment in time. This lessens its power over you.

———— ◆ ————

At the beginning of a client session, Jason told me about a pain in his back he had had for a few weeks. He was responsible for a big project at work and under a lot of pressure. He knew the pain was probably from stress, but getting a massage and going to the chiropractor had only provided temporary relief.

I invited him to close his eyes and describe the sensations. Was the pain sharp? Dull? Still? Pulsing? Describing the pain put him into an observer mode. Then I suggested that he might want to let the pain know he was aware of it. He said this felt silly, but silently said to the pain, "I feel you." As soon as he did, the pain lessened some. He stayed in this mode of observing and communicating with the pain as a witness to it. Suddenly he understood that he had been in denial of an issue at work because he was afraid to speak up about it.

We then worked on a good way for Jason to speak up at work along with some of the tools I will offer in the next chapter for calming his nerves. His pain lessened that day and stopped altogether once Jason communicated with his boss.

———— ◆ ————

I understand that you may not be used to tuning into your body and naming specific sensations, and certainly not communicating with them. You can start by recognizing that *something* is there, *some* kind of sensation, and acknowledge *that*.

SIX

You Are in Charge — Managing Fear in the Moment

I am going to give you three techniques that you can use in any situation when you experience fear or stress. The goal is to stay present with your fear in a way that lets you be in charge of your experience *and* utilize the information your fear response is giving you.

Remember, your body responds to messages from the emotional brain. **You can reverse this process by using your body to send messages back to the emotional brain that lets it know that you are safe.**

These exercises will help you calm your nerves quickly. They do this by releasing the energetic charge that is concentrated in the *upper* part of your body and moving energy down into the *lower* part of your body. This movement of energy signals the brain to turn off your nervous systems alert signals, stopping the flow of adrenaline and other survival chemicals.

The goal is not to rid yourself of the fear, but to be in charge of it, so you can think clearly and handle the situation in the best possible way. The fear will then diminish or go away naturally.

Tool #1: Deep Breathing

Have you ever thought you lost your wallet or your phone, and you got really anxious, only to find it a minute later? Or you thought, "Oh my God, my car's been stolen!" Then remember you parked in aisle E, not aisle D? When you realize all is OK, you let out your breath with a sigh or sound. That is your body doing what comes naturally to release tension. So, this tool is just doing the same thing intentionally.

You may be familiar with the idea of taking a deep breath to calm yourself. But what most people do it take a big breath in then blow it out in a quick burst. The problem with this idea of *taking a breath* is that the focus in on breathing in, not out.

However, the key is to make sure you exhale more slowly than you inhale.

Try the following:

- First, notice your present state of being, especially any tension you are feeling in your body. Observe your breathing. What is it like? Is your breath deep or shallow?

- Put your hands on your belly and imagine breathing into your hands as you inhale deeply. And exhale. Notice how you exhaled.

- Now, as you inhale count to three and as you exhale count to five. Inhale (1, 2, 3) exhale (1, 2, 3, 4, 5). Inhale (1, 2, 3) exhale (1, 2, 3, 4, 5). Inhale (1, 2, 3) and exhale (1, 2, 3, 4, 5).

When you breathe deeply and slowly, it moves your diaphragm in a way that activates the vagus nerve, which is the longest nerve in your body and a key player in your Autonomic Nervous System. The vagus nerve sparks the parasympathetic part of your nervous system, the part that calms you down. This slow exhalation sends a message to the emotional brain that you are safe.

Tool #2: Moola Bunda

This powerful technique is named after a Taoist term that has to do with activating the root chakra of security and belonging.

Whether you believe in chakras or not, this is great to do when you are nervous or anxious about doing something that scares you, even when you want to do it; like giving a presentation, participating in an important meeting, or asking someone for a date or a raise.

I used to teach acting and I would teach my students to do this before performing. They had great success booking more jobs when they did this before an audition.

You will want privacy when you do it. You may feel silly at first. If you do not have privacy, as with all techniques, you can do this in your imagination. The body does not know the difference between imagined experiences and actual ones. Although, I recommend doing it literally, to imprint the experience in your body, before doing it in your imagination.

If you can, do this with me now. If not, it's simple enough to do on your own later:

- Stand up with your feet hip distance apart. Take a moment to notice how you feel. Become aware of your body.

- Put your hands on your hips and rotate your hips in a circle in one direction, eight to ten times, as if you are spinning a hula-hoop around your waist. Sense energy flowing down into the lower part of your body as you move around and around.

- Stop and notice how you feel.

- To have some fun with it, you can do the hula-hoop movement again, this time make an "ah" sound that starts low in volume and gets louder and louder as you rotate around. Let it build until you are ready to release it by thrusting your hips forward and saying "Boom!" Something like "ahhhhhhhhhhhhhhHHHH-HHHHHHH BOOM!"

I use this tool before speaking engagements when I can slip into a bathroom stall or some other private place. Of course, I do the "ah boom" silently then! Women find this especially empowering, particularly if you identify as an introvert.

Tool #3: Tennis Anyone? or The Three Balls Technique

This is great to do when in public because no one will know. It is also good to do when you feel any sense of powerlessness, or when you are in the presence of someone who intimidates you. In this process, you will bring your awareness to three areas in your body: the balls of your feet, your ovaries or testicles, and your eyeballs. (If you are missing your ovaries, you can simply put your focus where they would be.)

I want to say a quick word about the pelvic area of your body. In spite of how openly sex is depicted in music, TV shows, and movies these days, we live in a world where sexuality is highly compartmentalized, judged, and distorted. For the most part, sexuality is associated with the sex act, and not as an aspect of our totality as gendered beings. While I cannot speak with absolute authority for men's experiences, I do know that many women - when in a state of fear or anxiety - feel cut off from the lower part of their body and their sexuality. This, in turn, cuts us off from our embodied power.

Whether you are a woman or a man, this technique is a way to become more connected to the embodiment of who you are, which is always going to help you feel more grounded and confident.

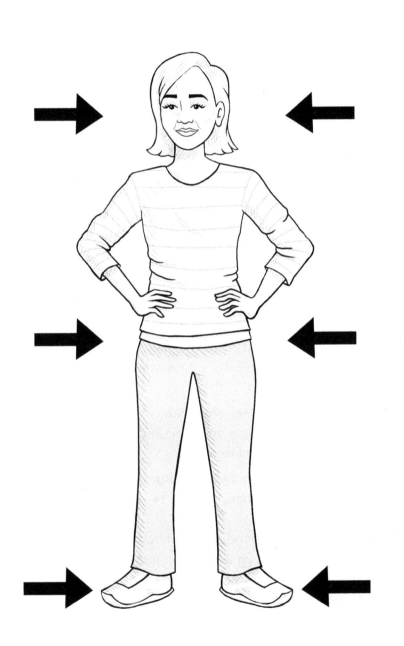

Do the following:

- Start by sensing your feet. Notice the sensation of your shoes, or whatever is covering your feet, and the ground or floor under you. Now focus your attention on the balls of your feet. This is the padded area on the bottom of your feet between your toes and arches. Put all of your focus there. Allow your feet to surrender to the floor.

- Sensing the balls of your feet, now, allow your awareness to include your ovaries or testicles. Sense a connection between the balls of your feet and your ovaries or testicles. See if you can sense a flow of energy between them. If you do not feel anything, that's OK. This can take practice. It may feel good, or it may feel a bit strange if you are not used to energy flowing through your legs. Just stay present with your sensations.

- Now, include in your awareness your eyeballs. Not your whole eye, just your eyeballs. Sensing, or imaging the flow of energy between your eyeballs and your pelvis.

- Now sense the energetic connection between all three places in your body: your eyeballs, your ovaries or testicles, and the balls of your feet.

- Notice how you feel now. Notice how your body aligns in space. Did your upper body shift slightly backward or forward? Do you feel more relaxed?

- Notice whether or not you are more aware of the room you are in, and any other changes.

I suggest practicing this often until it becomes quick and natural to do. You may want to put up a post-it to remind you. It could just say 'Tennis' on it. If someone asks what it means, you can say you have been thinking about taking tennis lessons.

SEVEN

What Was I Thinking! Mental Techniques for Managing Fear

When fear is present, it is important to pay attention to your thoughts. You need to become aware of the messages your mind is giving you. *Then,* decide if those thoughts are serving you. Are they what you want to believe?

We all have certain thought tendencies. Samantha was a big worrier. She often imagined that others were thinking bad things about her. When in truth, she was thinking bad things about herself. A number of my clients have had the habit of second-guessing other people's opinions of them, spinning various scenarios in their head instead of being present with what was actually happening.

They all had habits of thinking, born out of past experiences, that perpetuated an often subtle state of fear.

So let's look at your **fear-induced *thinking* tendencies.** First, we are going to explore whether your thoughts are usually oriented towards the past or the future. You may not be immediately aware of what your tendency is because so often thoughts come from the subconscious mind. For the most part, unless we pay attention, we are only conscious of a fraction of our thoughts. Even if you are very aware of your thoughts you may feel helpless to do anything about them.

When you become familiar with your thoughts, you will most likely see that they tend to give you the same core messages over and over again. I am now going to briefly speak on both future and past thought orientation. Note what resonates with you most. Then, I will give you a very simple technique to work with managing your thoughts.

FUTURE ORIENTATION: This is when your thoughts conjure up worst-case scenarios. Carol often made decisions impulsively without thinking of the consequences. When she became more aware of her thoughts, they were all oriented towards the future. Chief among them, "What if I never have a loving relationship? What if I never make the kind of money I think I should? What if I don't lose weight?" What if, what if, what if. Her fear of the future was so terrifying that she often made choices that would actually make what she feared more possible. She came to realize that underneath it all was a fear of dying alone.

PAST ORIENTATION: For others, their thoughts are on the past. Steven had overcome a lot in his challenging life. He was smart, ambitious and very capable. But he kept getting bogged down in the business he had started. His thoughts went like this: "I wasn't successful before. I never made big money in the past, so why do I think I can be successful now?" "I messed up." "That was a bad choice." "I shouldn't have spent that money." "I should have taken that business course."

Whether you refer to this as your inner critic, negative ego, inner gremlin or whatever, it is triggered by fear. Our thoughts are telling us we are inadequate, flawed, undeserving . . . some core message that says it is not going to happen now because it did not happen before.

I have a theory based on my experience about future and past orientation. This is not grounded in science, so please do not take it at face value. Test it; see for yourself if it applies. Here is what I think. If your thoughts are oriented toward the future, it indicates that you do not trust the outside world. If they are oriented to the past, it indicates that you do not trust yourself.

What resonates with you? What is your tendency?

I will now offer three exercises to choose from. You can do them all or just the ones that speak to you. These will help you get really clear about your thinking habits, your Modus Operandi. They will help to disempower the debilitating impact of habitual thinking that does not serve you.

EIGHT

Three Exercises for Thought Awareness

Here are three things to do to bring consciousness and change to your thinking.

Process 1: Assessment - Future or Past?

What are some common worries you have?

- Get some paper and write at the top: 'THINGS I FEAR' and set a timer for 5 minutes. Then start writing, and do not stop to think. I recommend a stream-of-consciousness writing. The point is to get out of your rational mind and access your subconscious mind.

- Just dump. If you cannot think of anything write: "I don't know what to write" until something comes. Do not pause to think. Keep going until the timer goes off. If you still have more to write, set it for another five minutes, and continue.

- Put what you have written away for a few hours or a day. This is symbolic of having kept these fears in your subconscious mind. Then take out what you have written and read it slowly. Highlight, or circle, anything that really stands out. Notice if there is a theme and if your fears have more to do with the future or with the past. It will not necessarily be one or the other. This is simply a way to begin to recognize how your thoughts contribute to your fears.

- Take what you have highlighted and write a single paragraph, condensing the information. Note what the core messages are. Usually, our fear thoughts are very repetitive.

- If you want to take it to the next level, see if you can discover the beliefs that support these fears.

In Chapter 11, I offer a guided meditation at the end of the chapter to help you change any beliefs you discover that do not serve you. There are many ways to change beliefs, and the scope of this workbook does not cover them all.

Process 2: With a Little Help From My Friends

If you are in an intimate relationship or have one or more close friends you trust, let them know that you are working on diminishing your fear thoughts. Ask them if they would be willing to give you feedback about what they notice. Here are some suggested questions you can ask them:

- *How often do you think I worry about things?*

- *Do I seem more worried about future events, or do I worry about current matters based on issues from my past?*

- *How do I express my fear? Am I direct? Do I express what I am really anxious about? Or, am I indirect. Do I dismiss people or situations, giving excuses or procrastinate about things?* If they aren't sure, ask them if they would mind paying attention and let you know what they observe.

- If you are close enough, you may want to ask them to point out to you, in a kind way, any patterns they recognize you exhibiting that you seem to be unaware of. You just have to promise to try to not be defensive when they do what you ask. This has worked really well for my husband and me to be able to be a mirror to each other about habits we have that do not serve us.

Process 3: Personifying Your Inner Fear

You are not your thoughts. The intention of this process is to help you separate from your habitual thinking. Once you know what the key messages are, imagine there is an internal part of you that is generating these thoughts. You are going to personify the source of these thoughts by imagining it as a person, an animal, a creature, or symbol. It may be that there is an inner child or adolescent that is producing the thoughts. These are parts of yourself that have not fully integrated into your adult self. For example, clients have personified this part of themselves as a dark cloud, a shy child, a snake and an uptight school principal.

When you can personify habitual thinking that does not serve you, it makes it easier to separate out from those thoughts and the beliefs that cause them, and stop believing those thoughts.

In the next chapter, I offer a short guided meditation so you can personify and communicate with your inner fear. It can be a very liberating process.

NINE

Personifying Your Fear Meditation

Suggestion: If you do not have the audio version of this manual, you or someone else can record the following meditation for your use. You can also find an MP3 of this meditation on my website: joieseldon.com/emotionsmanual.

During this meditation, don't worry about whether you see a clear image or not, just sensing it works. What you feel is more important than what you see.

Find a quiet spot and sit with your back straight. Close your eyes . . . become aware of your breath . . . relax your feet and legs . . . relax your hands and arms . . . relax your neck and throat . . . relax your shoulders and chest . . . let go . . . relax your stomach and belly . . . let your torso relax. Notice your breath.

- Take a moment to think about the kind of thoughts you have when you worry or you are stressed or anxious.

- If you were to personify the source of those thoughts, what kind of person, animal, creature, or image would it be like? Without effort, let an image come of someone or something that personifies that inner voice. Accept the first image that comes and imagine it in front of you.

- If no image comes, what kind of image would you imagine it to be?

- Does it have a mood or attitude? Is there a shape, color or tone to it?

- Once you have a sense of this part, in your mind say "hello" to it.

- Notice if it responds to you. Ask it, "Who are you? What is your purpose?" It may not communicate in words, so be open to whatever you get. Listen with your whole being.

- Is there something else you would like to ask it? Ask now.

- Let it know you heard what it communicated.

- Now, let it know that what it has been doing is not working. Ask if it is willing to help you in a different way, a better way.

- Whatever its response, tell it how you would like it to treat you. Notice how it responds.

- Whether or not it has agreed to change, let it know that you recognize that it has worked very hard and that it deserves a vacation. Assure it that you are not getting rid of it. You are simply letting it go on a vacation for a while.

- Now see or sense this personification moving away from you. It is going further and further away from you, back and back, until it is gone.

- Notice what it is like to have it gone.

- Sense yourself sitting in the room you are in, and when you are ready, slowly open your eyes.

Now that you have this personification, whenever you notice thoughts in your head that don't serve you, those patterns of thinking that are so familiar, you can imagine this being and talk to it. Let it know that what it is saying is not really helping, or that you choose something else. Or, simply acknowledge its presence and feel it separate from you. Send it off, or see it fading away. You may want to write about your experience.

TEN

Getting in Touch with Hidden Fears, a Writing Exercise

Earlier, I talked about the common symptoms of unconscious fear and asked you to note what came up for you. If you took notes, this is when we will work with them. Either way, pick one thing you to work with now. You can repeat this writing exercise as often as you want.

Common symptoms of hidden fear:

- Procrastination: what are you putting off because of fear?

- Excuses for why you are not doing something you say you want to do.

- Lack of relationships and/or lack of intimacy in your relationships. You may have many different feelings about it, so just focus on fear for now.

- Feeling isolated or lonely.

- Feeling stuck.

- Anything else you would like to work with.

The Exercise

- Get a stack of paper or a notebook.

- At the top of a page, put the symptom, for example: "I

procrastinate taking action on my business." "I lack intimacy in my life." "I feel stuck."

- Start writing stream of consciousness style, whatever comes up. Do a brain dump of anything and everything you can think of. Making sure to include what you fear around the subject.

- Next, go over what you have written. I recommend allowing some time between the writing and the review so you have a fresh eye.

- After reading what you have written, distill it into a paragraph expressing the core fears. Then, as best you can, distill the paragraph into a sentence or phrase where you define what your main fear is. (For example: "I am not in a relationship because . . . I will be hurt/they will find out how flawed I am/I will become mean and controlling/I will lose myself in the relationship." Or, "I am stuck in my career because . . . I don't deserve to succeed/ I'm not smart enough/I'm not talented enough/if I ask for a raise, I'll be fired.")

Once you have clearly defined a core fear, you can do the guided meditation that follows to help release that fear.

ELEVEN

Releasing Fear - Guided Meditation

Suggestion: If you do not have the audio version of this manual, you or someone else can record the following meditation for your use. You can also find an MP3 of this meditation on my website: joieseldon.com/emotionsmanual.

During this meditation, do not worry about whether you see clear images or not, it is OK to just sense them. What you feel is more important than what you see.

Sit comfortably with both feet on the ground and your back supported. Take a deep breath in . . . exhale. Take another breath . . . exhale. Imagine a chord of gravity attached to your tailbone. Let any tension in your body flow down this chord into the earth. Take another breath . . . exhale . . . Bring your attention to your third eye, the area between your eyebrows.

- Imagine you are sitting in a small theater and there is a movie screen in front of you. On it a film begins to play. It is what you fear. You may see other people including yourself, or just yourself. See or sense what you fear actually happening. People may be telling you things or may behave in certain ways. Engage your senses. Feel the feelings that come as you watch what you fear taking place.

- Now, freeze the film. See it stop, and the frozen image on the screen. Now, imagine the screen is self-destructing. See it heating up, it is beginning to melt, parts catch on fire. It is falling, melting. Watch the image disintegrating until it is all gone.

- Now, See a new screen. Imagine what you want to happen. A new film starts. See yourself doing thing the way you want to, being the way you want to be in the world. Confident, energized, easeful. Imagine the results you want, what you are doing, or having what you desire. Sense or see that image playing before you. Now feel what this is like in your own being. Become that image on the screen. What is your mood? What thoughts do you have in this scenario? What does your body feel?

- Keep this feeling going as much as you can as you slowly become aware of being in the room you are actually in, slowly opening your eyes, seeing things around you feeling as if this movie is true. You have what you want now. You are who you want to be. Keep this feeling going as long as you can.

TWELVE

The Dynamic World of Anger

Welcome to the glorious and powerful emotion of anger.

Poor anger; it has a bad reputation. That is because it is often misunderstood and misused. We are told that it is a negative emotion, that we should contain it, get over it. Many people are afraid of it. Then there are people who get angry at the drop of a hat, and those who allow their anger to escalate into rage, believing that they have no control over it.

My intention in this chapter is to demystify anger. I want to offer a new perspective that will help you utilize the valuable message of anger, and at the same time reduce aggression, conflict, and stress in your life. Let's start with the fundamental purpose of anger.

The function of anger is to protect you. On a primal level, it protects your life as the fight instinct of the fight-or-flight response. In modern society, it has evolved to become a different kind of protector: one that protects your autonomy, your self-identity, and your right to be who you are and to make your own decisions. Anger's core message is "No! This is not OK with me. I do not want this."

Anger can keep you from being taken advantage of physically, psychologically, and emotionally. It is your automatic boundary-setter. It is activated when someone steps over a line and says or does something that threatens you, your values, or your integrity. You need something that moves you to say "No, you can't treat me this way!" That something is anger.

A major aspect of anger is the physicality of it. As I said in the segment on fear, when the sympathetic part of the autonomic nervous system is activated, your body gets ready for fight-or-flight.

In both anger and fear, you experience muscle tension and stress hormones. While fear's energy is contracting and *inward moving*, anger's energy moves out from you towards the object of your anger. The secretion of adrenaline, cortisol and other powerful hormones charges you with energy, particularly in your upper body. This outward movement of energy and focus, combined with the strong physical charge, potential volatility, and unpredictability, is what makes anger so challenging to manage.

Typical physical sensations are clenched teeth, tight jaw, increased heartbeat, or feeling hot inside. If you are especially angry, your hands may form into fists, or you may want to strike out or throw something. We see this behavior in animals. Gorillas pound their chest or bare their teeth, dogs growl or bark, cats hiss and swipe at you.

Managing the powerful physical activation of anger is going to be key in learning how to experience and express anger in healthy ways.

With each emotion, there is a range of intensity of feeling. The degree to which you become angry will vary based on the specifics of the situation. A coworker telling you a white lie that has minimum impact on you might be annoying, whereas having a trusted loved one betray you could be enraging.

Anger is an appropriate response when someone deceives you, tries to control or manipulate you, or judges you in a way that attempts to degrade or diminish who you are. Sometimes anger is a reaction to circumstances in the world that do not directly affect you, and over which you have no control, but that goes against your values and principles. Politics and religion can evoke this type of anger.

You may be thinking, "I never get angry." Over the years I have had many people tell me that. What I say to them is, "I'm sorry, but I don't believe you." Once they come to understand what anger is about, and recognize they have a judgment of anger as being bad or wrong, they inevitably say something like, "OK, I do get angry, and in fact . . . " They then proceed to tell me all the things they are angry about.

One of the great gifts of anger is that it can provide motivation and energy for change, whether it is social injustice, or something very personal. When something is happening in your life that you are no longer willing to tolerate – such as habitual behavior that limits you, money problems, unhealthy relationships, or a job you hate – then feeling the anger that prompts you to say "no!" to those conditions can motivate you to change your circumstance.

It can be a wonderful antidote to hopelessness or debilitating fear. On more than one occasion I have overcome feelings of hopelessness by getting angry and saying, "I will NOT fail!"

Sometimes, we get angry at ourselves. A word of caution: when you are angry at yourself, particularly when you are not living up to your own expectations, it is important to notice if your anger at yourself is motivating or denigrating.

Punishing yourself with anger does not motivate you, any more that it does an employee being browbeaten by an angry boss. I know, I have tried punishing myself many times and it never works. However, there have been times when I have sat in front of a mirror, looked myself in the eye and said, "No more! I see what I am doing and I do not want to be this way. I can change."

When this is done from a place of self-love, or at least self-respect, it can be powerful. When done from self-hate, it can take you down.

I will be addressing the problems with anger, but first, it is important to realize that when you experience anger consciously, as a primary emotion, it can be clean, clear, concise and powerful. Optimally, it is a way that you respect yourself by saying "no" to something that you know is not good for you.

To help you gain a new perspective on anger I will speak to three points: some misconceptions about anger; the difference between anger as a primary emotion and the secondary use of anger as a defense against feeling vulnerable and powerless; and healthy ways for you to manage your anger without stuffing it or being overwhelmed by it.

THIRTEEN

Three Misconceptions About Anger

The first misconception many people have is equating anger with aggressiveness or confrontation. They believe that expressing anger means yelling or fighting, or that someone will get hurt. Associated with this belief is that once you feel angry, you will have no control over it.

I have had a number of clients who had a parent or former partner who expressed anger as rage. They were afraid to let themselves feel their own anger because they did not want to lose control and hurt someone the way they had been hurt. Some had declared that they would never be like "him" or "her," so they stuffed their own anger in the name of being loving.

There are some circumstances when we need to be forceful, where aggression is called for. Even rage can be appropriate in a life-threatening situation. However, anger is about setting boundaries, it is not about being destructive. Most of the anger you will experience in your life can and should be communicated without confrontation.

One reason we association anger with aggression is because the strong physical charge of anger is an *outward moving* energy. It is always directed at someone or something.

What has been your experience of anger in the context of aggression or confrontation? Have you been hurt or frightened by someone else's anger? Or perhaps you have hurt someone with your own anger. If so, know that you can learn a different way to express yourself and to defend yourself.

We humans have evolved physically, intellectually, and technologically. But emotional evolution has been lagging, particularly when it comes to anger, and it is time to bring more consciousness to this core aspect of who we are.

In a civilized society, aggression should be a last resort rather than the first response. This does not mean you should never be forceful, or passionate in your expression of anger. I am not advocating for passivity, not at all. I will say more about this in the section on managing your anger.

For now, what is important to understand is that when you are present with your anger and its message, you can be in charge of it. You can choose how or even if to express it. In many circumstances such as at work, it is not safe or appropriate to openly express anger. That does not mean you have to stuff it. Anger's core message is about setting boundaries, not about being destructive. One of the most effective ways to communicate anger is to be grounded and calm when you say "no" to whatever it is you do not want.

The second misconception is that anger is not spiritual. With the very positive intention of promoting good will among people, religious and spiritual teachings can directly or indirectly portray anger as something good people should not be feeling.

You cannot dictate which emotions you will or will not feel. You are not bad or wrong for feeling anger. There is a wonderful essay by Robert Augustus Masters called "Compassionate Wrath: Transpersonal Approaches to Anger," in which he explores the positive use of anger as a spiritual teaching tool. I have included a link to this article in the bibliography.

——— ◆ ———

Just as we need to have boundaries and say no to others, we need others to set boundaries and say no to us. It helps us to grow as human beings. One thing I am grateful to my husband for is that he has never been afraid to call me on my stuff. Coming to marriage in my mid-forties, I had a lot of strong opinions about how things should be done. Sometimes I was very judgmental of my husband and he would get angry. His anger was firm but never abusive. By expressing his anger, he taught me humility and to be less judgmental. I saw how I was treating him the way my mother treated my father, and I sincerely did not want to do that. I can only imagine that if my father had stood up to my mother in the same way, how much better off my whole family would have been. I will be outlining some tools for communicating anger a bit later.

———— ◆ ————

The third misconception is that anger is bad for your health. There are studies that show a direct correlation between anger and heart disease and other stress-induced illnesses. I do not dispute that. However, this leads many to believe that *all* anger is bad for your health.

The problem with this assumption is that it encourages people to suppress or deny their anger. They think, "I don't want to feel something that's bad for me!" When you resist your anger impulse, you push it underground, where it taxes your immune system and results in chronic tension. This creates toxicity in your body and in your relationships.

Repressing anger, or any emotion, takes a certain amount of life-force energy to hold it in place; energy that could be put to better use. The trick is to feel your anger and process it quickly, so the charge of it passes with minimum impact.

There is a massive lack of understanding and negative judgment against anger throughout the world, causing people to misuse it. Most people do not know how to express it cleanly or process it in healthy ways when expressing it is unsafe or inappropriate. I believe it is *mismanaged* anger that can impact your health.

Stuffing your anger, allowing it to escalate, staying righteously angry, or getting stuck in it where you ruminate about something over and over, *that* is what produces excessive stress on the body. If you have been angry about something for a long time something is amiss.

Primary anger, in and of its self, is not bad for you.

You may want to take some time now to think about your own assumptions about anger before moving on to the next chapter.

FOURTEEN

Clean Anger vs. Defensive Anger

We have just looked at some misconceptions about anger. Now, I want to clarify the difference between anger as a primary emotion, what I refer to as "clean anger," and anger as a secondary emotion used as a defense against other feelings you do not want to have, ones that make you feel vulnerable or powerless.

Remember, anger is a primary emotion that protects your autonomy, your Sense of Self. Of all the emotions, the experience of anger can be the most complex because your Sense of Self is complex. It includes your beliefs, attitudes, past experiences, and unexpressed emotions. It includes your family and cultural influences and the social and economic environment you grew up in. The level of your self-confidence, self-esteem, and self-worth are all part of your Sense of Self and dictate how you react to things. Anger is there to protect all of that. No wonder it is so complex.

With all that complexity, anger can be a powerfully transformative emotion. No matter how difficult your history or current issues, anger can cut through to the truth.

Secondary Defensive Anger

All too often, the anger we experience in ourselves and coming from others is not anger as a primary emotion; rather it is anger as a secondary emotion that is used as a defense against other feelings we want to avoid. They are either feelings we are afraid will be too painful, such as sadness or shame, or feelings of powerlessness or vulnerability.

This kind of anger is still saying "no" to something, but that something has to do with what is inside you.

Some extreme manifestations of this defensive anger are domestic abuse, gang violence, and even terrorism. Where you see this more readily in daily life is what is generally referred to as "being defensive." I want to illustrate this with a couple of stories.

———— ◆ ————

Brian started a home improvement project but after a couple of weekends, he stopped working on it. His wife would ask, "When are you going to finish it?" And he would snap back, "I'll do it! Don't worry about it." Brian had taken on a project bigger than he felt capable of completing, but he was embarrassed to admit it. He had started it in the first place because they could not afford a contractor. Now he felt stuck and ashamed that he didn't make enough money to hire someone to do the work. His angry response was a defense against his feeling of shame.

Whenever Trudy had tech issues on her computer at work, she would get very, very angry. She would rage at the computer. Her level of anger was way out of proportion to what was happening. In truth, her anger was against her own feeling of powerlessness. She had grown up with very controlling parents, so this was a big trigger. Rather than feel the discomfort and vulnerability of feeling powerless, she would get angry. This is anger as a secondary emotion. When Trudy realized her current triggers were linked to her past, she was able to catch herself, calm down, and get the tech support she needed. She even learned to figure out solutions on her own, which gave a sense of personal power.

———— ◆ ————

Defensive anger is a lot easier to see in other people than in our self! Yet, when you are really honest with yourself you can feel and know the difference between "clean" primary anger and defensive anger.

For most of us, secondary anger manifests in a subtle way – a stubborn clinging to and defending of an opinion or position, blaming others for our problems, keeping people at a distance, or becoming obsessed with a certain issue that we are righteously angry about.

————— ♦ —————

Growing up, Theresa had been treated very badly by her mother. Now approaching fifty, she was still angry and could list all the things her mother had done to her – or had not done – that she should have. She had lots of casual friends, but no one close. She was lonely. After expressing anger about her current life, she would sometimes cry. I noticed that I did not feel moved by her tears, which led me to think that they were about something else.

What ultimately came to light was that the anger she was expressing was actually a defense against feeling deep grief. Grief is about loss, and her loss was not having the kind of mother she wanted and needed. When she finally allowed herself to feel her grief, I was deeply moved. As she became more present with her true emotions, the anger dissipated. Her ability to express grief allowed her to move on from her childhood wounds and her long-held anger.

————— ♦ —————

I want to end this discussion of clean anger vs. defensive anger with an illustration of clean anger. I was teaching an ongoing class in presentations skills, and one week three people had canceled the day before the class. I was not happy about it, but it happens, and they had given me the required 24 hours notice. I still had several other students coming. Then, 15 minutes before the class was due to start, I got a call from yet another student saying she had double-booked herself that night and was not coming.

Instantly, I felt tension in my body, then heat rising in me. I was angry.

In the past, I would have taken my student's carelessness personally, assuming that she did not value me or the class; that I was somehow inadequate – all thoughts stemming from a sense of powerlessness. My reaction might have been to say with force, "What do you mean you're not coming? How could you do this to me?!"

Or, as I so often did, I would have tried to hide my anger, and been covertly hostile, or what is often referred to as passive-aggressive behavior. "Well, I wish you had called sooner, but I understand," I would have said, in a tone of voice that would convey that I did *not* understand. She would have felt yucky. Later she might have unconsciously come up with a good reason for not coming back to class. I would have remained angry at her forever, and that night I would have carried the energy of my unexpressed anger into the class.

This kind of communication is akin to playing the martyr. *"I will sacrifice my own feelings in order to be nice to you."* The implication is that my feelings are less valuable than yours, which I would have then resented, adding fuel to the fire.

What I did instead was this: I felt the anger energy running through my body. I took a breath without speaking, allowing for a moment of silence. Then, calmly, yet firmly, I said, "While I understand your dilemma, you made a commitment to be here and you're calling me 15 minutes before the start of the class to say you're not coming. That is not appropriate and it doesn't work for me." To which she replied, "I'm really sorry. I screwed up. I don't know what else to do." I said, "I understand. And you are going to do what you need to do. Just know that it is unfair to me for you to call at such a late hour to cancel."

After a moment of silence, she told me that, unexpectedly she had her 16-year-old daughter with her and asked if could she come too. I said, "Yes, bring her." They must have flown because they got there on time. The class turned out to be a breakthrough experience for both of them

It was not necessary for me to say to her, "I'm angry at you," and it would have been inappropriate for me to raise my voice. In contrast, because my husband and I have an explicit agreement (meaning we have talked about it and agreed that it is OK to express the energy of our emotions with each other), we have both said, "I'm angry," with a certain amount of force. This is also clean anger, as long as we are not blaming or punishing each other with our anger.

———◆———

Take a moment now to see if you can discern on a visceral level – that is, the feeling *in your body* – the difference between clean, primary anger, where you are setting a clear boundary, and secondary defensive anger, where you are covering up other feelings. Using your imagination, how might they feel different in your body?

Now think of how you typically experience anger. You may notice that in some circumstances or with certain people you are very clean, but with others, your anger is mostly defensive.

Do you fear anger? Or maybe you claim to never get angry. More than any other emotion, anger is the one that clients most often deny feeling. Then, when we explore further, it turns out they have plenty of anger, but they are either afraid they will hurt someone, or they will get in trouble for it. In the end, when they finally experience their anger, they inevitably gain insight and grow emotionally.

FIFTEEN

The Relationship Between Anger and Safety, Shame, Depression and Food

Before moving into the exercise section, I want to say a quick word about four things that can impact your experience of anger.

1. **If you are someone who has a lot of stored up anger because you did not feel safe in expressing it in the past, I want to acknowledge that releasing old anger can be scary.** When I discovered how much anger I was carrying from my past it was terrifying. I could not shake the feeling that if I expressed it out loud, I would literally destroy whoever or whatever was in front of me. It took time, but releasing old anger was tremendously freeing and well worth the effort. I will be offering ways for you to process your anger that is *safe*, as well as liberating.

2. **Defensive anger can be an attempt to cover up toxic shame.** Healthy shame is basically remorse. We experience it when we have done something that hurt someone or went against the values we believe in, and we feel bad about it. You have hurt someone and you feel truly sorry. You can then apologize, or make amends in some way.

   Toxic shame is not a primary emotion. It stems from a false belief that something is fundamentally wrong with you. With this belief, it seems as if there is nothing you can do about it.

If you suffer from a sense of being flawed as a person, know that this is absolutely not true. Getting in touch with your anger and saying "No" to the shaming messages you got will help you to move through it.

3. **A word about depression**. Some define depression as anger turned inward, and in many circumstances, I believe that is true. However, it is far too simple a statement for the complexities of the broad spectrum of different manifestations of depression. First of all, severe clinical depression and bipolar disorder are not simply repressed anger. They have a biochemical component and must be treated with the seriousness they deserve.

   Then there is temporary depression caused by a sudden shift in expectation. We expect something to happen and it doesn't. You believe you are going to get the raise, the new job, the house you bid on, and you don't. For a few minutes, hours, or days you feel let down. This is a natural response to disappointment. If it goes on for very long, then something else is happening that needs to be addressed.

   Still, there are many people who suffer from depression due to suppressed anger. In particular, it is most often a habitual suppression of big and small angers that you are afraid you will get in trouble for. In essence, what is happening is that so much psychic and physical energy is used to suppress the anger, that it depletes you of your vitality, and the results appear as depression.

4. Finally, **there are physical things that affect our mood**: foods we eat, especially sugar, caffeine and alcohol; hormonal shifts, such as the one women experience during menstruation; and imbalances in the body due to lack of exercise. These can all impact your emotional state and can make you irritable, moody and prone to anger. If you have chronic anger issues, I highly recommend getting nutritional advice and support, as well

as having your hormones tested. This goes for men as well as women.

As we approach the final segment on managing anger, know that suppressed and denied anger can manifest itself in a variety of ways including dysfunctional relationships, isolation, and loneliness, passive-aggressive behavior, depression or a variety of illnesses. Suppressed anger can be just as destructive as excessive overt anger that goes unchecked.

If anger is an issue in your life, learning how to access your anger and to be in charge of it, instead of *it* being in charge of *you*, may be the most powerful thing that you can do to create the life you want.

In the next chapter, I offer tools and techniques for improving your relationship with anger and managing it in daily life.

SIXTEEN

Boundaries — The Heart of Anger

Remember, anger is the emotion that lets you know when someone has crossed a boundary. It protects your Sense of Self. Healthy boundaries allow you to manage and express your anger appropriately.

It is easy to recognize physical boundaries. You know it is not OK for someone to touch you against your wishes, or break into your home and steal your personal property.

What can be harder to recognize are energetic boundaries.

Energetic boundaries are a fundamental aspect of self-development. As an infant, you experienced no distinction between yourself and others; all were one. Boundaries came into place as you began recognizing that you were a separate individual. That was the beginning of the universal and lifelong process of creating a Self and then learning how to be that Self. Energetic boundaries define and protect that Self – who you are.

This boundary is not metaphorical. It is literally the emanation from your body of what scientists call bioelectromagnetic energy. This energy not only runs your bodily functions, it emits an energetic force field that surrounds you. With awareness and intention, you have the ability to manage this energy to protect yourself physically, emotionally, psychologically, and spiritually. Your values, beliefs, self-image, and the very essence of who you are, are all protected by your energetic boundary.

Your boundaries have a profound impact on your relationships, and your ability to function in the world.

How well your energetic boundaries function is dictated mostly by your subconscious mind. However, when you have greater awareness of your boundaries, you can then be in charge of what kind of boundary you want to have, with whom, and in what circumstances.

Four Boundary Styles

To help you discern what your own energetic boundary is, I will define four general styles. These are not meant to be exclusive or definitive, but rather to set a context in which you can begin to recognize your own boundary mode. You may have a degree of or combination of these in different situations or around different people. Notice which ones you relate to most:

Style #1: **HEALTHY** – A healthy boundary is one that is strong but flexible, firm when needed and relaxed when safe. With a healthy boundary, you do not accept abuse in any form, and you are able to have healthy intimacy in a relationship. You are able to make choices that maintain a certain level of balance in your life. You listen to your feelings and intuition when making decisions.

Style #2: **UNCLEAR** – If you are someone who does not have clear or strong boundaries, your tendency may be to go along with whatever is happening, to automatically say yes without thinking. You may have vague or codependent relationships. You may not be aware of your own needs or wants. You agree to things, and later wish you hadn't. You let others make choices for you or tell you what to do. You may tolerate insults or abusive behavior.

Is this you? Take a moment to think about what the consequences are of this boundary style. How do you ultimately cope? Do you stuff your feelings about things until you explode at the person you resent? Do you stuff your feelings until you are ill? Or perhaps you stop responding to phone calls or emails, effectively cutting people off without stating why.

If someone is invading your space, as you move through the rest of this chapter, look at how you can change that; how you can utilize anger, in a workable way, to set clear boundaries.

Style #3: **RIGID** – This is a tight, closely held boundary. It is hard for you to soften or allow yourself to be intimate with appropriate people. You have a hard time letting go of things or letting others praise, love or nourish you. Isolation is a symptom of this type. You lack friends, or intentionally keep people from getting too close to you.

If you are not letting people in, that is an indicator that you have work to do in this area. It is too complex a topic to cover thoroughly in this manual because everyone has unique reasons why this protective strategy developed. However, this entire manual is a resource for changing this dynamic. Know that you can change this, and the payoff will be more than worth the work.

Style #4: **WIDESPREAD** – You may have a strong boundary, but it is cast wide. You are easily affected by your surroundings and other people's behavior. A high level of sensitivity or taking things too personally may be a symptom of this type. You may have an overactive sense of responsibility, where you try to fix or control other people's behavior. Or, you get upset because others do not behave the way you want them to.

————◆————

This used to my boundary style. I first became aware of it in a graduate school Somatic Psychology class. In a demonstration, I stood on one side of the room and the professor stood on the opposite side, with his profile to me. Then he turned towards me. Before he could take a step in my direction, I flinched. He pointed out that because my body moved instantly, it meant that my energetic boundary was quite far away from my physical body.

That somatic exercise taught me that my boundary was wide-spread. Inside my energetic boundary were my neighbors, my city, and sometimes even across the continent from me – Washington, DC. I found myself in a constant state of vigilance and anger at certain neighbors, at politicians, and at injustices throughout the world. The list was long. In short, I was taking too many things too personally, and as a result, I was angry pretty much all the time.

I realized I had to reel in my energetic boundaries and manage my energy. I began practicing in my car. Naturally, I was hyper-critical of the way other people drove. Whenever I caught myself raging at other drivers, I would imagine the body of my car as my boundary. Instantly, my attention came into the present. I no longer cared about what anyone else was doing, and my anger stopped immediately.

———— ♦ ————

Some common behaviors that indicate boundary issues are: saying yes when you mean no, or no when you mean yes; not making or keeping agreements; not being able to keep secrets; frequently running late; ongoing resentment or obsessive thinking about other people; and having a strong emotional reaction to things that are out of your control.

Developing Healthy Boundaries

Developing healthy boundaries starts with awareness. I invite you to be curious about what kind of boundaries you have. Pick one or more days when you are going to pay close attention to your energetic boundaries. Make sure you track it in different settings with different people: with family members, co-workers, customers, your significant other, and friends.

Notice body sensations, as well as your emotional responses, to people and situations. Pay particular attention to any subtle or clear feelings of anger. See if you can determine which of the four categories describes you most. You may have different boundaries in different situations. Sometimes we can have clear boundaries at work, but with our parents or siblings, we have no boundaries or very rigid boundaries. I recommend journaling about your experience.

One goal of this work is to support you in accessing your innate wisdom and instincts to help you discern how your boundaries are operating in your life. As you grow in emotional intelligence, you will naturally develop healthy boundaries.

Before moving on to healthy ways to communicate anger, I want to share a couple of thoughts.

First, boundary issues can be internal as well as external. Whenever you are being harsh with yourself, or self-punishing, you are crossing an internal boundary. It is good to be self-discerning, to tell yourself hard truths. But when your self-criticism is denigrating, you are not holding clear boundaries of what is and is not OK. If someone else said mean things to you, you would be upset. Yet many of us say mean things to ourselves on a regular basis. Things like, "I'm so stupid. I'm such a loser. I'm hopeless. I'm unlovable." Having clear internal boundaries allows you to be honest with yourself without punishing yourself.

Second, not only do boundaries keep out people and experiences that hurt you, they create a container in which you can be your most authentic self. Having well-defined boundaries provides a safe space in which you are free to listen to your inner guidance, to create, and to express yourself. Master Qigong teacher Vicki Dello Joio says, "Boundaries let you be who you are, and they let others see who you are." Her book, Way of Joy, which contains more wisdom on boundaries, is listed in the bibliography.

The ignorance and disregard of boundaries are evident in issues ranging from personal relationships to global conflict. With all that is going on in the world today, the premise that good relationships depend on good boundaries is monumentally evident. Look at world conflicts. They all stem from disregard of boundaries, from a government to its people, one government to another, one tribe to another, one religion to another, one gender to another. Instead of praying for world peace, I think I will pray for good boundaries.

SEVENTEEN

Guides for Managing Anger in Daily Life

We have looked at some key misconceptions about anger and clarified the difference between anger as a primary emotion and as a defense against feeling vulnerable or powerless.

I will now offer you a variety of tools and techniques for:

- Getting in touch with the physical manifestation of anger.

- Evoking and releasing hidden or suppressed anger safely.

- Managing anger in present time without stuffing it or being overwhelmed by it.

You do not need to do all of the exercises, choose what speaks to you. However, I urge you to start with body awareness, for without learning to recognize and tolerate the charge of anger in your body, the rest will be far less effective.

Once you have gone through the exercises, feel free to adapt or combine them in any way that works best with your sensibilities.

Body Awareness

We have some very interesting expressions in the English language that refer to anger. Blow your top, up in arms, hopping mad, on the warpath, all indicators of the physicality of anger.

I cannot emphasize enough that a big part of managing anger is in your ability to stay present and grounded when the charge of anger hits your body. Common physical manifestations of anger are heart pounding, increased blood pressure, muscle tension, especially in your neck, jaw and upper body, revved up energy, a narrowing of focus, and feeling heat. (Perhaps you have you heard the phrase, *"My blood is boiling."*)

We each have our own particular temperament, which is impacted by childhood experiences. You may be more or less prone to anger than others. My husband is a naturally calm person, whereas I can get angry all too easily.

Before delving into the tools and techniques, it is important for you to be clear on how anger manifests in *your* body, so you can stay in charge of your anger, instead of it being in charge of you.

Exercise 1: Child's Play — Acting "As If"

This is an exercise you can have fun with. You are going to act as if you are angry, without worrying about whether or not you have a genuine experience of anger. Just pretend. Acting as if you are angry wakes up your emotional body and lets it know that, yes, it is OK to feel angry.

You will never be able to utilize the benefits of your anger if you are unwilling to feel it in your body. I know I keep restating this, but it is so important. If you have believed that anger is bad, you may have suppressed the sensation for so long that any expression of anger will feel over the top.

Have courage. Do this alone, where no one will see or hear you. You may feel silly, and that is OK. There is no need to be precious with this exercise. I give you permission to do it badly! You may just find it quite liberating.

If you think of something that makes you angry, it is fine to work with that. But, it is not necessary. For now, I want you to practice being angry.

Do this now:

- Tense your upper body, your jaw, neck, upper arms, and back muscles. Make fists with your hands.

- Make an angry face. Narrow your eyes, feel tension in your face. Exaggerate your sensations.

- Now say *"NO!"* Say *"NO!"* again, and put energy into it. Use your voice as much as you can. Put your hand out in front of you with palms facing forward. Thrust your arms forward, like you are pushing something away, and say *"NO! NO!"*

- Exaggerate your anger. Say: *"I'm angry. No! I don't want this. I don't like this! This is not OK with me! I'm angry!"*

- Notice how your body feels. Notice your breath.

- Now, let it go, shake it loose. Take a big breath. Exhale. Relax.

- Notice how you feel now? Do you feel more energized, or less?

Take a minute to write down your observations. Consider answering these questions:

  » Was it fun or scary to express your anger?

  » Did you feel any genuine anger?

  » If it was hard to do, why do you think that is?

This is all information about how you relate to anger.

Exercise 2: Self Observation — Being Present With Anger

There are two ways to become familiar with how you deal with anger using self-observation. You can do one or both of these exercises.

Sometimes, when people do these exercises, they have realizations about themselves that make them uncomfortable, or they judge themselves as wrong or bad. This is not the intent of these exercises. To keep that from happening, I recommend that you set an intention to learn and grow from the observation, and to have compassion for yourself and others. The best way to accomplish this is to adopt an attitude of curiosity, to become a witness to your own behavior.

Once you commit to observing yourself, here are two guides to help you with the exercises. One is the **ANGER MONITORING CHEAT**

SHEET, a list of seven questions you can ask yourself to help you focus your observation. The other is **SEVEN ANGER STYLES**, which can help you identify your tendencies.

————◆————

Anger Monitoring Cheat Sheet

- Where in my body do I feel anger most?
- On a scale of 1-10 how strong is my anger?
- Is my anger clean, or a defense against other unwanted feelings?
- If it is defensive, what is the emotion I don't want to feel? (i.e. shame, sadness, fear, powerless, hopeless, etc.)
- What am I saying "no" to?
- How did I handle my anger? (i.e. express it, notice it without expressing it due to the circumstances, ruminate about it, stuff it, etc.)
- If I wish I had handled it differently, what would that look like?

————◆————

Seven Anger Styles

The Temper Tantrum – The person who is easily overwhelmed by anger. Children are good at this, but some adults do this as well.

The Attacker – Someone who has an intent to punish others, such as the boss who manages by yelling, or the spouse/partner who demeans their significant other.

The Volcano – Someone who holds in his or her anger, suppressing it over and over again until they spew out a tirade when the proverbial straw breaks the camel's back.

The Wall – This person does not acknowledge their anger, and instead becomes stoic and uncommunicative. They tend to hold resentment.

The Passive-Aggressor – The person who gets angry but won't express it directly and instead become snarky or sarcastic. Also known as covert hostility, this is a tactic commonly used by martyrs.

The Discharger – Quick to anger and very expressive - though not necessarily directed at others - then moves past it quickly.

The Clean Anger Person – Someone who recognizes his or her anger and expresses it appropriately. They set clear boundaries, resolve issues without blaming or punishing others, and communicate feelings in a workable way. They are open to hearing and receiving anger from others. Someone who is OK with just feeling anger when it is not appropriate to directly express it.

--------◆--------

Part One: General Observation

Make a commitment for the coming week, or for at least three days, to pay close attention to your anger and keep a journal of your experience. If you are someone who gets angry often, picking a single day to track your anger may be enough. Make sure you track it in different situations: at work, at home, in social settings, and so forth. Pay attention to both clear and subtle experiences of anger.

In particular, notice if you are aware of the initial spark of anger. Or, do you find yourself in the full state of anger before you know what happened? Try to become aware of the earliest possible physical sensation that lets you know you are getting angry. Then notice your thoughts, for example if you are taking things personally. Use the Anger Monitoring Cheat Sheet for further insight.

Part Two: Focused Observation

If you have an upcoming event where you anticipate possible anger, or you have an ongoing situation or relationship with someone that pushes your buttons, pay attention to your interactions in the same approach as Part One. This does not have to be a monumental situation; maybe there is someone in your life that merely annoys you.

Again, take the attitude of being an observer of your experience. Notice what happens when you are about to be in the situation or with that person. Notice your body sensations and your thoughts. Try to stay present with your experience throughout the interaction. Make notes of your experience afterward using the Anger Monitoring Cheat Sheet.

Self-awareness is the first step in increasing your emotional intelligence. When you have a clear picture of your own behavior, you will know more specifically what you want to work on, if anything. Now let's look at ways to process and communicate anger.

EIGHTEEN

Communicating Anger

Given how charged anger is, how do you communicate it effectively, without getting into an argument, or the other person becoming defensive? You cannot control other people's responses, but there are things you can do to make it safe for them to hear your message. Making people feel safe is the key to reducing defensive reactions.

In order to consciously create safety for others, as well as for yourself, it is important to know what kind of relationship you have with the person you want to communicate with. I don't mean whether or not you are siblings, partners, or friends. I mean, how much permission do you have to express your feelings honestly with that person. We have conscious and unconscious, spoken and implied agreements as to what is okay to say with everyone we come in contact with.

Agreements are mostly unspoken and often unconscious. Yet, just like energetic boundaries, they exist. In fact, agreements are an inherent aspect of boundaries.

In order to recognize what kind of relationship you have with someone, we will look at three basic levels of communication agreement. I will briefly state these levels and then go into specific ways to express yourself on each level.

Level One is when there is no agreement or permission to express anger. Level Two is where it is OK to talk about your anger or other emotions without expressing the energy of it. Level Three is where you have permission to express the full energy of the emotion, as long as you treat the other person with respect. Let's look at each of these levels and how you would deal with your anger in each of them.

Level One: You're on Your Own — Managing Anger Without Direct Expression

Level One is where there is no agreement or permission to express anger. These interactions are typically with strangers, people you do not know well, or someone you know to whom it is not safe to express anger. Unfortunately, family members can fall into this last category, where expressing anger to an abusive, controlling, or otherwise dysfunctional parent, sibling or spouse can have negative consequences.

It is easy to think that not expressing an emotion is the same thing as repressing it. Not so. Suppressing your anger can lead to resentment, or ruminating on a situation, where you go over and over what you wish you had said or done. It can lead to depression, or sudden lashing out at people you feel safe enough to express yourself to without being abandoned. In other words, you are dumping your feelings on innocent people. This is a common experience in families.

You have also sent a message to your psyche that feeling anger is not okay, reinforcing the neural pathways in your brain that are conditioned to respond to feelings of anger by suppressing it.

Here is a way to stay silent without stuffing your feelings. This approach is actually quite simple, but it can take practice to build this muscle. This same skill can be used in all situations, whether or not you have permission to express your anger.

The key components are:

- Staying present with body sensations.
- Being an observer of your experience.
- Paying attention to what your anger is telling you.

First, become aware of your breathing and be willing to be quiet for a moment. Notice sensations in your body. It can help to think of anger's charge as red energy flowing throughout your body. Send this energy down into the lower part of your body. Know that you have the power to use that energy to handle the situation. It helps to get in touch with your feet and lower half of your body.

As much as you can, become a witness to your experience and the situation. Depending on what is happening, you may have to stay present with your feelings and process it later. What you ultimately want to be aware of is whether your anger is a clean anger, or if is it a defensive anger that is triggered by a sense of powerlessness or other feelings that you do not want to feel, like embarrassment.

Imagine you are shopping, and the sales person is on a personal call and not paying attention to you, you are in hurry, and you get angry. Instead of stewing and shooting dirty looks at the clerk, then later complaining to someone else, or stomping out of the store muttering curses under your breath, feel the energy of the anger flowing through your body. Feel your feet on the ground, and take a moment to recognize what you need in that particular situation. In this scenario, ask for what you want. "Excuse me," and in as neutral a tone as you can manage, look them in the eye and ask, "Can you help me?"

The clerk may sense your anger, and this is fine. In can be very effective to feel angry and speak in a calm voice. I find it gets people's attention without causing them to get defensive.

Remember, the purpose of anger is about honoring yourself and setting boundaries, not in punishing other people.

Creating Agreement

For the next two levels, it is beneficial to actually sit down with the people closest to you and talk about what kind of agreement you want to have with each other for expressing anger and, in fact, any emotion.

Agreements help us create a safe space for communicating with people that matter to us. We rarely if ever, talk about *how* we are going to communicate our feelings to the people close to us.

Start with the person you think would be most willing to discuss this. Tell them that you want to learn how to communicate more effectively and ask if he or she would willing to talk about what kind of agreement you can make for expressing feelings. I will give you an example of how to create an agreement in a moment.

Level Two: Talking it Out – Communicating with Words, but Not the Energy of the Emotion

This is appropriate when you have *some* level of agreement, spoken or implied, to talk about your feelings without expressing the energy of them. Depending on the situation, this can include co-workers, employees, friends, neighbors, siblings, and even romantic partners where you do not yet have agreement to fully express your anger. If expressing anger is difficult for you, this would be a good way to begin.

Any approach to sharing feelings goes best when you ask the other person if it is OK to share your feelings. Asking permission shows respect for their boundaries. It goes a long way toward creating safety for the person you are angry with, as well as for yourself.

If you do create an agreement to share feelings, the conversation would be simply to let them know you have some anger you would like to talk about and ask when it would be a good time to do so.

If you do not have an explicit agreement, the conversation would go something like this:

"I have something I'd like to talk to you about. Would that be OK?" They may ask what it's about. You can say something to the effect of, *"I have some feelings that I'd like to share with you. If you can't talk right now, when would be a good time?"* If they want to know more, you can say, *"I have some anger I would like to talk about."*

It is important to communicate with a calm voice. If they express apprehension, you can say, *"I'm not going to yell at you. I care about our relationship. It's important for me to communicate what's going on with me."* When you do talk, in a calm voice explain to them why you feel angry. It is important to own your own feelings, and not say "you made me angry." You can say something like, *"When you did such and such (or when such and such happened), I felt angry."* Then say why. *"I felt disrespected,"* or unacknowledged, or left out, or whatever it is that your anger was saying no to.

However they respond, really listen. Feed it back to them in your own words. You can say something like, *"Let me make sure I get what you're saying,"* and then say what you heard.

If they get defensive, remind them that they said it was OK for you to share and do your best to work through it. Whatever the outcome, thank them for listening when you are done.

Real communication takes time. We have egos, insecurities, and what a teacher of mine used to call "automaticities" — our ingrained habits of defense. I have had discussions with my husband that took a few days to process. We would talk, then a day or two later one of us would go to the other and say, "I understand now what you were saying, and I realize what was really going on with me."

———— ♦ ————

One of my client's best friends used to copy everything she did to the point of buying exactly the same car, right down to the color. My client was very angry about it, but she was not someone who expressed herself easily. She felt like she had to end the friendship. We did some role-playing on how she could express herself safely. She was able to get agreement from her friend to talk, and they set a date to discuss her feelings. Instead of ending the friendship, as she had feared, it deepened it. Her friend revealed her own insecurities, and they were able to be more honest with each other from that time forward.

———— ♦ ————

Level Three: Letting it Rip, with Grace

This is where you get to express the full energy of your anger. For you, this may be good news, or it may be terrifying. Since this level of expression is based on your level of agreement, there will probably be very few people in your life who fall into this category. However, it is important to have at least one relationship where you can fully express the energy of your anger. When you have even one person with whom it is safe to express yourself fully, it does something to your psyche. It gives you permission to be yourself, to have your feelings without being judged. I cannot emphasize the importance of this enough.

What makes this work is having a clear agreement with that person. Tell them you want to have safety in expressing yourself, and you want to give them permission to express themselves in ways that are healthy for both of you.

You can share with them what you have learned about anger in this manual. Ask them if they are willing to make an agreement about how each of you can express your anger to each other. If they are not open to full expression, start with a Level Two agreement.

If they agree to full expression, set your guidelines. Here are my recommendations.

1. Agree to ask permission each time you want to express your anger. It might sound like this: *"Friend. I am feeling angry, can I express it to you?"*

2. Agree to use "I" statements. Rather than saying, "You made me angry when you didn't do what you said you'd do." Say, *"You didn't do what you said you'd do, and I'm angry about it."* Notice the difference in the tone.

3. Agree that if one of you expresses anger without permission, that person will take responsibility for the impact.

———— ◆ ————

What I discovered from having this kind of agreement with my husband, where both of us can express our self fully, is that I have learned a lot about myself. Sometimes my anger was righteous, and sometimes my perception of what had happened was way off. But by releasing the energy of my anger it cleared the air in a way that I could then see where I was wrong. This builds trust in a relationship. Sometimes we've actually ended up laughing after expressing ourselves vociferously. After twenty-three years together, we no longer ask permission. We are at the next level. Which is that we have absolute trust and respect for each other. We know each other so well now and accept each other as the imperfect people we are.

NINETEEN

Getting Rid of Old Anger

If the idea of releasing old unexpressed anger seems daunting to you, know that I will not suggest that you go to people from your past and "let 'em have it" (satisfying as that might be). However, I *will* be offering a writing exercise and a guided meditation.

While these exercises are under the heading "old anger", they can also be used for current anger if you are unable to express or communicate it because it is not safe to do so.

These are great ways to release long-held anger at a person, a group of people, an organization, or any entity. Old anger often shows up as resentment or depression. Unprocessed anger can kill your inspiration, your creativity, your self-esteem, and more. I urge you to be honest about any anger you are holding from the past and give yourself permission to express and release it.

Exercise 1: The "Screw You" Letter

This is one of my favorite processes to do. By the way, you will not be mailing this letter.

Get a pile of paper or a cheap notebook. Set your intention to rid yourself of old anger and resentment, *and* with no harm to the person you are addressing.

Write "Dear (So and So)," then let it rip. Write all the things that you would love to say, but would never say to their face. Let it come stream-of-consciousness style. Don't worry about punctuation. Let your feelings flow. If all you write for a page or more is "I hate you!!!" or "Screw you!", that is OK. But do find some words that express *why* you hate them.

Do not be concerned with being politically correct, or try to be "spiritually conscious" or understanding. This is pure energetic charge being expulsed from your psyche.

Keep writing until you feel spent. Then put what you have written away somewhere — in a drawer, behind some books, in a box. Tuck it away. This is symbolic of having stuffed these feelings for so long.

The next day, take out the paper and write some more until you are spent again. You may notice there is a different tone this time, or not. I often found that the second day I was less charged, and consequently more articulate. Then, sign the letter and tuck it away again.

On the third day, take it out and read it, all of it. Then destroy it in a ritual of your choosing. I always burned mine, but you can shred it or rip it up. If you have a compost, put it in the compost to help something healthy grow. Whatever your method, hold a conscious intention to let go of your past anger.

You may need to do this for many people or more than once for a particular person. When I first started doing this I wrote a letter to every member of my family, then one to the whole family as a group. I even wrote one to God, expressing my disappointment in my life not turning out the way I wanted it to.

At the end, feel the feelings of freedom, of being done with that anger.

Exercise 2: The Big Dump Meditation

The intention of this exercise is to release anger that you have not been able to let go of. I will describe how this simple meditation works, then you will need to do it on your own because this is primarily about you expressing yourself. It is good if you have a place that is private, sound-wise, so you can speak out loud. Speaking out loud makes it more real, more tangible. If you have no other option, speak the words in your mind.

Sit in a chair. Do not do this lying down. Close your eyes and think of a person, a group of people, or an organization you are harboring anger towards. Imagine who or what you have chosen to work with sitting two or three feet in front of you. Set an intention to rid yourself of anything you are carrying from the past. Then, make the statement, "With harm to none." The purpose is not to punish people, but to release yourself of the burden of your anger.

Begin expressing out loud, or in your imagination, all of the anger you feel towards that person or group. Do not hold back. Swear, curse at them, be as ferocious as you feel. No need to adhere to the "when you did this, I felt angry" statement. They are not going to hear you so let it out.

Do not try to be an evolved spiritual being. You may very well have a full understanding of why the person hurt you, but that does not mean you have released your anger. I have had many clients who truly understand why their parent, friend, or ex behaved they way they did. But they are still carrying the pain and impact of those people's behavior. That is what needs to be released energetically. I want to be clear that this is not simply venting. There must be an intention to release the old anger and to be done with it.

As you express your feelings, you are going to see or imagine your words as debris piling up between you. As you speak, sense the pile between you growing higher and higher until you cannot see the person any longer. Keep expressing the full energy of your anger until you feel done, complete. Now you have a pile of your expression between you and the object of your anger. Then, imagine a fire hose washing the pile of spent anger away, until there is nothing between you and the object of your anger. You can also sense fire coming out of the hose if you want and burn the debris away.

Finally, sensing the person or group across from you, release them by saying, "I let you go." Imagine them disappearing or receding into the distance until they are gone.

Now, feel yourself free of the anger. Imagine a stream of golden light coming down from above, through the crown of your head, filling in the spaces where your anger used to reside. Feel the sense of comfort this light provides. Surrender to the safety of this feeling.

When you are ready, open your eyes and notice your surroundings. Take your time. You may then want to write in your journal.

You will need to find a quiet spot where you will not be interrupted for at least 15 minutes: if there is a lot of anger, it could take longer. This is an exercise you can repeat as many times as necessary with one person who you have a lot of anger at, or with different people.

TWENTY

Beautiful Sadness

The Value of Sadness

Sadness is a profoundly beautiful emotion and far more indispensable to your wellbeing than you may realize. The primary purpose of sadness is to help you recognize loss and then process it.

At its heart, sadness honors the connections in your life. We humans are social creatures. We are hardwired to connect to others. It is key not only to our survival but to our happiness. We need other people in our life, and we need to have a sense of belonging. Our need to belong prompts us to develop attachments to people, pets, places, and things. **Sadness helps us process the loss of connection.**

The degree of sadness you experience can range from momentary wistfulness to deep grief. The depth of your sadness is determined by the degree of importance and value of whoever, or whatever, you have lost.

Yet sadness is often viewed as merely something to get over. In the stoic western culture, when a loss occurs that is not tragic, the emphasis is on getting past it and moving on with your life.

With the best of intentions, others may try to diminish your loss, or encourage you to "be strong," "buck up," or feel better. Yes, it is important to not wallow in sadness, which of course it is not healthy, but too often people will try to dismiss it as if there is something wrong with feeling sad.

There are two key blocks to sadness. The first is the belief that sadness is somehow negative, or it means you are weak. This is evident in the attitude that men who cry are not manly, and women who cry easily are dismissed as being *too* sensitive or "just being emotional."

The second block is a fear of being overwhelmed by sadness, and feeling embarrassed or vulnerable. Like a client I will call Terry, who had not cried in years in spite of having suffered profound loss. She was afraid that if she let herself really feel her grief it would take over, and she would never stop feeling sad.

Sometimes there are tragic losses that do take time to move through. With the exception of a tragic loss, sadness is not an all or nothing experience. One of the primary goals of this work is to help you be in charge of your emotions, and not let them be in charge of you.

When you are present with your sadness, even a profound one, you can function in your life, do the things you need to do, like go to work and interact with others, even laugh; then come back to a full experience of your grief when you have the space and time to do so.

Of course, not all losses are worth tears, sometimes a mere few seconds is enough to move through it. But when we fail to acknowledge our sadness, its essence will show up in some form or another.

Your Body and Sadness

To have a greater understanding of how sadness functions, let's look at what happens on a physical level.

Your energy is low, muscles are lax, and your movements are slower than usual. Your chest may cave in a bit, shoulders rounding as if protecting your heart. You may or may not have tears, but your visual focus softens and turns inward. Your body is turning your attention away from the outside world and towards your inner world in order to give you time and space to process your loss.

The physical manifestation of sadness varies in intensity and duration based on the value and attachment of what has been lost. If the loss is sudden and of high value, like when a loved one dies unexpectedly, you may initially feel very activated, with a pounding heart and strong body sensations. You are in a state of shock. Eventually, though, the low energy and turning inward will come.

Although there are basic body processes that go on for everyone, each person has his or her own unique experience of sadness. You may feel sadness primarily in your heart area, and someone else may feel it in his or her stomach.

You may cry easily, or like Terry, never cry. This may have to do with your temperament, or you may have learned early on to stuff your sadness. It could also be physical. Did you know that men's tear ducts tend to be larger than women's? A man may feel sad and even well up but not actually cry simply because his tears ducts are big enough to contain his tears.

Our emotional responses are always subjective, so your physical experience of sadness is influenced by your nature and by your beliefs and attitudes about sadness. Is it something you welcome, or do you resist it?

It is easy to recognize big grief, but you may have more loss in your life than you know. It is the small losses that will most easily go unprocessed and will build up a reservoir of sadness that zaps your vitality.

I want to help you discern the more subtle experiences of sadness that often go unrecognized or are dismissed.

The Difference Between Feeling Your Sadness and Denying or Suppressing It

What happens when you do not fully feel the sadness within you? Your ability to function is diminished. Because you experience low energy with sadness, it is common to interpret it as just being tired.

Terry would often begin a session saying how exhausted she was. However, once she started to experience more of her sadness, and subsequently other emotions, she felt energized.

One way to identify unprocessed sadness is to notice if you are feeling apathetic. When asked for an opinion or given a choice, you may respond with "I don't know," or "I don't care," or "whatever."

I do want to say that sadness has its own timing. Other emotions are meant to come and go quickly, but sadness takes its time depending on how strong the connection or deep the value of the loss. In the case of a big or tragic loss, the period of mourning may last for some time. The more consciously you feel this, the more you will be able to function in the world and continue with your life, which is different from "getting over it."

When someone we love dies, years may go by and something, like an anniversary, will remind you of that person and you will feel sad. This is because that person still has value to you. Sadness comes and goes. This is normal.

Sometimes sadness is misinterpreted as depression. Though the slowing down and turning inward may feel similar, they are not the same. This is an important distinction. When the primary emotion is sadness, feeling it will move you through it. If you are depressed, feeling sad may actually perpetuate your depression if not done with support from a health care professional.

As I said in the chapter on anger, other than diagnosed clinical depression or bi-polar disorder, depression is often the results of suppressed anger, or anger turned inward.

Sadness can feel scary to get into because it also takes you inward. It wants you to look at what you value, to be present with your heart, your caring, your love and your loss. It leads you to actually experiencing your sense of separation, which is a very intimate experience. You may think, but why would I want to experience separation!? First, because it is the truth of what is happening to you, and being truthful with yourself is a source of true power. Second, because without that experience you would not value connection in the way it is meant to be valued.

Conversely, sometimes we think we should be sadder than we are about a loss. After speaking at an event, a woman in the audience shared with me that her mother, with whom she was very close, had died recently. Everyone around her was expecting her to basically fall apart. She was sad, but she had had such a great relationship with her mother, and she had had time to fully prepare for her death. She told me I had given her permission to be true to herself and not feel guilty that it was not what others expected of her.

Unlike other emotions, you may feel sad sometimes for no apparent reason. In these times, simply feel the sadness without trying to analyze it. It is coming from some deep part of yourself. If you trust your body's wisdom and let yourself feel sad, you will probably know why. But even if you don't, feeling it moves the energy through your body and you will ultimately feel better.

Sometimes a good cry is more about releasing stress than actual sadness. Scientific studies show that tears of sadness are chemically different than stress tears. We may even cry when great things happen, especially when unexpected. Then we have tears of joy.

Three Types of Loss

In order to better recognize loss, let's look the different types of loss. As you read the following, I recommend that you make note of any losses, memories, or thoughts that come up. You can use these to work with in the exercise section in the next chapter.

1ˢᵗ Type - The Loss of People and Pets

The first, and most obvious, is the loss of a relationship. When someone you love or who is important to you dies, or when a beloved pet dies, you of course experience grief. When a relationship breaks up, or a friendship ends, even if you wanted it to end, there is often sadness over the loss.

Our relationship with pets are generally pretty pure, and the grief we feel is straightforward. Human relationships, however, can be very complex. So it is common for other feelings to be present during a grieving process, particularly when a family member dies, a marriage or partnership is over, or a friendship ends badly. You may also feel anger, shame, or fear. You may even feel relief. It may seem incongruous to have these feelings *and* be sad. It is not only possible, but likely when the relationship is complex. I have lost both my parents and both my siblings, and with each loss, I experienced a different kind of sadness.

Take a moment right now and ask yourself, "Am I willing to feel my sadness?" Was your answer an easy yes, or was hesitation or tension in your body? If so, honor that hesitancy. Be curious as to what that is about. This is not a race to the finish; it is a process of becoming emotionally empowered. It takes time.

2nd Type - The Loss of Objects

The loss of a possession can have an impact ranging from a small yet lingering grief, such as when you lose a favorite pen, to profound grief when losing something big, like your home. Again, it has to do with the value and level of attachment you have to that object. It may sound silly to grieve the loss of a pen. And it would be if it were a freebie you got at the bank. But if it were the pen your father gave you when you graduated from high school because he knew you wanted to be a writer, that pen would have a lot of meaning to you and feeling sad over losing it would be totally appropriate.

Sometimes the loss of a possession is your fault, and it is easy to criticize or even punish yourself for losing it. If the loss is due to theft, anger may be your first reaction. In these scenarios, it can be easy to not recognize the sadness you feel. Why does it matter? Remember, unacknowledged emotions stay in your body and psyche until they are processed. Sometimes your sadness may last only a few seconds, yet it is still important to feel it.

3rd Type - The Loss of the Intangible

The third kind of loss is one that most often goes unprocessed because it is not recognized as loss. This is the loss of the intangible. This kind of loss can be small and fleeting or have a major impact on your life.

There are two basic kinds of intangible loss. The first has to do with **unmet expectations**, and the other has to do with losing **something you wanted but never had**.

Unmet expectations happen all the time. On a small scale, it can be as simple as the loss of a great idea. You thought of something brilliant and a minute later it is gone. "Dang, I just had the best idea. What was it?" It is your thought, so of course you expect to remember it. But you don't, and you feel let down. The degree of that let down is based on how much value you gave that thought.

You go to a dinner party expecting to have a fantastic time, but it turns out to be a snooze. In both of these scenarios, a common feeling is disappointment. At the heart of disappointment, you will most likely find sadness.

On the other end of the spectrum of unmet expectations is when you have a dream that does not come true. The loss of a dream is an important occurrence that often goes unprocessed. If the loss happens gradually over time, you do not recognize it as an event. You may be too busy trying to get past it so you can avoid the painful realization that you failed.

——— ♦ ———

When I was twenty years old I moved to Los Angeles with the dream of becoming a movie star. That dream did not come true. After years of intermittent success, a lot of "day jobs" and a gradual lessening of my ambition, it became clear that it was not going to happen. By then I had embarked on a personal growth path that ultimately led to my work with emotions. In some ways, it felt like a relief to give up the struggle to achieve something that clearly was not happening.

Many years later, my idol Katharine Hepburn died. I went into a deep state of mourning. It became clear to me that I was grieving more than the death of someone who was a huge inspiration to me; I was also grieving the loss of my dream of becoming a movie star.

——— ♦ ———

When sadness goes unacknowledged, it hangs about in your body and subconscious mind, draining you of energy and undermining new dreams. Time goes by and you sense a kind of dullness, a lack of energy or lack of confidence you once had. You hesitate to commit yourself fully to a new dream.

Most of us have experienced the death of a dream. When it became evident to my client Sam that his dream of becoming rich as an entrepreneur was not happening, he stoically told himself that he had failed and that he should cut his losses and move on. But, he was struggling with what he wanted to do, what kind of job he wanted. This is when he came to me.

What was holding him back was unexpressed sadness at the loss of his dream. Once he could release his held-in grief, he was able to see himself in a new light and inspiration began to flow. He realized that he had gotten caught up in focusing too much on the end results of becoming rich, rather than the expression of his passion and the process of what he was doing. He was able to look objectively at what had gone wrong with his business. Instead of feeling defeated, he became energized with what he said was "a more realistic point of view." Sam reordered his priorities. He scaled back his business and began again; older, but wiser.

———— ◆ ————

Now let's look at the **loss of something that never happened**. What I have found to be the greatest unprocessed sadness that people carry in them without realizing it is the loss of what they needed from their parents, but did not get. Love, attention, affection, understanding, being seen and heard, being validated for who you are – these are all spiritual needs. You may have a clear understanding of your family issues and what your parents did to you, or did not do *for* you. You may have shed many a tear over it and still not have actually grieved the loss in a way that lets you fully move on.

Consciously grieving loss of something you needed but never had provides a "missing link" in your development that you can do something about. When you can feel the sadness of an intangible loss, the stories you were told, or told yourself, about why this happened, drop away. Stories that say *there is something wrong with me; I must have deserved that kind of treatment.*

These stories come to a young mind simply trying to make sense of his or her reality. The sticking point develops when the story becomes a belief. Feeling grief becomes the very thing that can set you free from your debilitating beliefs.

Finally, in this category of intangible loss is the **loss of opportunities**. In your work, you may lose a client, a sale, or a promotion. That is when many people focus on what they did wrong, what they could have or should have done differently. You may get angry, or criticize yourself, but do you let yourself grieve the loss? I bet not.

You may think it is silly to grieve over not getting a client, and of course, you may not need to. The point I want to make is that loss is not an intellectual process. There are no shoulds or shouldn'ts. It is about being honest with yourself about what you are feeling. If you are carrying unprocessed sadness it can have a big impact.

Sadness is not a complex emotion. However when we do not acknowledge it, the consequences can become complex. Unexpressed sadness can keep you from doing what you really want to do. Because it turns us inward, it can also keep you from connecting to others, leading to loneliness and a lack of fulfillment.

A World Without Sadness

Think about what the world would be like without sadness. It would be a very cold world if we did not grieve our losses.

Sadness helps us delineate that which has value from that which does not. It honors those you love, and is an expression of who you are. I invite you to embrace the beautiful emotion of sadness.

TWENTY-ONE

Exercises for Processing Loss

The following exercises will help you understand your relationship to sadness. They will help you manage it when it comes up unexpectedly, or when you have to interact with others when sad. It will help you know the difference between sadness and depression or apathy.

Each exercise has its own chapter so that you can return to it anytime you want.

In this segment there are five exercises:

1. Write your sadness history. This is a quick way to get a big-picture view of how you relate to sadness.

2. A writing assignment to process past losses.

3. A guided meditation to release sadness from the past.

4. A noticing assignment as a simple way to become aware of present time sadness.

5. Sharing feelings with another person. This helps you become accustomed to feeling vulnerable with another person while expressing yourself.

The foundation for emotional intelligence is self-awareness and knowing your body is the key. As you do the exercises, keep track of the sensations you feel in your body.

TWENTY-TWO

Your Sadness History

It can help to take an objective look at your relationship to sadness. You can do this as a story, as if you are writing an autobiography using the following questions as a guide, or simply answer the questions.

- How did your parents express or suppress sadness?
- How did they respond to you when you were sad? Did you talk about it?
- What messages did you get directly or indirectly about sadness?
- How do you act when you are feeling sad?
- Where do you feel it in your body?
- What is your attitude towards sadness?
- What beliefs do you have about being sad?
- How easily do you share your sadness with others?
- What else do you have to say about sadness?

TWENTY-THREE

Processing Past Losses

Note: If you have a traumatic loss and have not really dealt with it, I highly recommend working with a professional therapist, a spiritual counselor or join a grief support group. I do not want you to be alone while doing these exercises and get triggered in a way that makes you feel re-traumatized or unsafe.

The point of this exercise is to have a contained way to access your sadness and get into it. Then to become an observer of that experience and discern what you value, and what habits or issues you have with sadness.

You will need a pad or stack of paper, pen and a timer. Think about someone or something you have lost in one of the following categories.

- People: What is a person or pet you have lost through death or the ending of a relationship?
- Objects: What is a tangible object you have lost that had great meaning to you?
- Intangibles: Is there a dream or goal you had that never came to fruition? What is it you wished you had had in your childhood, adolescence, or early adulthood?

Part One:

1. Write the loss at the top of the page.

2. Take one minute, no more, to think about that which is lost. Engage your imagination if need be to conjure it up.

3. Set the timer for 10 minutes.

4. Start writing stream-of-conscious style. Just let words come without care of punctuation or complete sentences. Do not stop and think. If words do not come write down, "I don't know what to write," or "I feel sad," over and over until words come. If nothing new comes after writing this down a few times, stop, but continue to be with the memory until the time is up.

If it is a big loss, and a lot of emotion comes, lots of tears, you may need more time. Reset the time for another ten minutes and be with the feelings. Continue to reset the timer if you need more time. It is important to keep setting the timer so you know you have a container, a boundary, where you can so, "OK, I'm done," or "That's enough for now. "

When you are done, take a break. Step away from your writing long enough to feel yourself fully in present time. Have something to drink. Stand up and move. If you can, step outside or take a walk. Take as long as 24 hours, but preferably not longer.

Part Two:

1. Read what you have written. As you read, notice any body sensation and what your level of sadness is, or if other emotions come. Notice if you feel as sad when you wrote it or has it lessened or increased?

2. As you read what you have written notice what values are evident that make you grieve these losses?

3. If you know there is more to feel, come back to it another time,

even later that day. It is important to practice being in charge of your experience.

4. You need not feel totally chipper afterward, but go on to do something else while honoring what you do feel. I recommend doing something physical. Do the dishes, pull weeds, sweep, walk around the block; anything to move your body and get your attention on something that grounds you in present time. At the very least, take a moment to look all around you. Notice details of what you look at, wherever you are.

TWENTY-FOUR

Releasing Loss

GUIDED MEDITATION: This meditation can be helpful in releasing losses you either pushed through or did not recognize as a loss, such as the loss of a dream.

Suggestion: If you do not have the audio version of this manual, you or someone else can record the following meditation for your use. If you do this, pause the audio whenever you need more time.

Think of a loss that you have had that you did not process or that you sense still affects you. It can be a tangible loss, or it can be intangible.

Sit where you can have your back fairly straight and supported, and have both feet on the ground. Take a moment to get comfortable. Notice your breath. Notice your feet on the ground and your legs. Simply notice any felt sensations.

- Relax your feet and legs, hands and arms. Notice your torso. Now bring your awareness to your neck and shoulders, your chest, stomach, and belly. Notice your breath. There is nothing to do here but notice and let go, allowing a gentle state of mindfulness.

- Now, imagine in front of you someone or something you lost, or something you feel sad about. What image comes to mind? Or, you may simply sense a presence.

- What meaning do you place on this loss? Do you blame anyone? If so, for the moment, set the blame aside, let go of that thought, and bring your attention to the loss itself.

- Notice what is happening in your body. What sensations are you aware of? Feel what you feel. It may be more than you expect, or it may be less. Accept what is.

- Is there something you would like to express to the person or thing that is lost? Expressions of sorrow, love, remorse, or even anger are welcome. In your imagination, take a moment now to express what you are feeling. Continue expressing yourself as long as it feels natural, until you feel a shift or release, or you feel tired. Take your time.

- Notice what it is like to express your feelings.

- Now, say to the image in front of you, your object of loss, "I let you go. I release my sadness." Sense the object of your loss, and your sadness, moving away from you. Sense them fading away until you are aware of sitting there alone.

- Take a breath. Become aware of your breathing. Whatever degree you were able to express yourself is fine. Simply notice what the experience was like. Was it easy, scary, hard or fulfilling?

- Become aware of your whole body now, aware of what you are sitting on, of your breath. Gently begin to move your hands and arms, your feet and legs a little bit, stretch.

- When you feel ready, gently open your eyes and notice the room you are in. Take time now to sit with what just happened. You may want to write about your experience.

TWENTY-FIVE

Acknowledging Loss in Present Time

Noticing

Set a day where you are going to pay particular attention to loss. I recommend doing this on two different days, setting an alarm to remind you to check in once every hour or two. They need not be consecutive.

Notice losses around your work, your family, and yourself. They may have to do with:

- Relationships

- Tangible objects

- Intangibles, such as the loss of

  » ideas

  » opportunities

  » unmet expectations

You can also track awareness of past losses that show up. If you keep a journal, you can use it to write down your experience.

TWENTY-SIX

Sharing Your Feelings
with Another Person

This is important because it will help get past the awkwardness of expressing yourself when you feel vulnerable:

Sharing with a Neutral Person

Think of someone you feel safe with - a friend, a family member you trust, a spiritual counselor or therapist. If you are reaching out to a friend or family member, ask if you could share some feelings with them. Be clear that the feelings are not about them. You can say, *"I'm working on my emotional intelligence,"* or *"I'm processing some old feelings and I need someone to share them with."*

When you get their permission, share your sadness as honestly as possible. See how present you can stay, even when it is uncomfortable, to feel your feelings in their presence – whether in person or on the phone.

If there is no one in your life with whom you feel safe, I encourage you to either find a therapist or join a therapeutic group where you can practice expressing your feelings with someone else.

Sharing with the Person You Feel Sadness About

If you carry sadness about someone still available to talk to, consider sharing your feelings with that person, if it feels safe enough to do so. Again, I recommend asking permission, only letting them know that the feelings have to do with them or with your relationship with them. People are most receptive when they feel respected and safe.

When sharing, make your statements about yourself, not about how they *made* you feel this way. For example, *"When we broke up, I felt so sad. I know I was very angry, but I was also very sad about it. I just wanted you to know."* Or, whatever is appropriate for the circumstance.

It may feel incredibly vulnerable. What I have witnessed, and experienced myself, is that being vulnerable with someone can be a transformative experience.

TWENTY-SEVEN

Joy — The Fuel for Success

The fourth and final foundation emotion is Joy. At last, a happy emotion!

Part of what makes joy wonderful is that it is so pleasurable. However, joy is much more than pleasure, more than happiness or excitement. In this segment, we will explore the deeper meaning of joy and how you can cultivate it in order to have more ease and fulfillment in your life.

Joy is the emotion of connection. It is what you experience when you feel connected to yourself, to others, to nature, to Spirit, or simply to life itself. It is a state of flow, free of judgment and resistance.

Other emotions have either an inward or an outward moving direction of energy, but Joy is omnidirectional. It radiates out in all directions.

While other emotions prompt you to specific kinds of action, joy is a dynamic state of being that fuels your personal power in a way that allows you to take the actions you want to take more freely.

It is the fulfillment of preferences and potential. Falling in love, making love, getting your dream job, receiving something you really want, accomplishing a goal; these are all joy-inducing experiences. They may seem to be just about being happy or excited. However, what is happening is that you are either feeling a connected to another person in a meaningful way, or you are connected to yourself through the fulfillment of your desire.

We all have individual preferences. I feel joy walking in nature, dancing or listening to music that I love; while others are joyful at a ball game or meditating. I happen to love public speaking and always feel joy doing it. Others hate speaking in public, but love solving puzzles or math problems. In each case, the joy comes from the fulfillment of individual preferences.

Another key aspect of joy that surprises some people is that it is not simply the absence of other emotions. Joy can include the experience of any other primary emotion, including sadness, fear, and anger. Because when you feel any of these genuinely, you are experiencing a connection to yourself. You may not feel happy or excited, but the emotions will have a particular quality of flow or spaciousness to them. You will be less attached to them. And, they will move on more quickly. This will make a lot more sense when you work with this material.

What has been a revelation to me is that by cultivating my ability to experience more joy, I can manage challenges and solve problems far more easily. And, I am having a lot more fun

When you are feeling joy, there is no separation between you and what you love, need or want. Its message is, *in this moment you have fulfilled your potential*. Notice I said, in this moment. Feeling joy 24/7 is not the goal. Being human is a complex experience, and you need all of your emotions to navigate life's journey.

Too often we focus on problems and how to fix them. When you are overly focused on what is not working or what is lacking, you keep yourself in a state that cuts you off from joy. When you are cut off from joy, it limits what is possible for you. Joy provides greater access to your creativity, your innate intelligence, and your intuition.

Where you can go amiss is to believe that because you did not get what you wanted, you have failed and are not deserving of joy. What works better is to listen to the other emotions that arise, and use them to help you take an action that will either let you release that wanting for appropriate reasons or do something that will bring what you desire closer to you.

Increasing Your Capacity for Joy

Patricia came to me when her second marriage ended. She had a history of severe depression and felt herself wanting to withdraw from life, as she had done in the past. This really scared

her. She now had to support herself and was afraid of losing her job.

She was highly educated, very intelligent, very creative and had many interests. She had been in therapy twice and found it helpful. She was very aware of her issues and unworkable coping strategies. So, what was the problem?

She did not know how to feel joy. Her brain and body were conditioned to respond to the life-long stress and hurt she had experienced by withdrawing, or in other words, disconnecting. In order to change this pattern, I told her she needed to create an experience of something other than fear and pain, and thus interrupt her impulse to withdraw.

She could experience joy in certain moments – when she was in nature, or engaged in a creative project, things she did by herself. But, experiencing joy while she was self-aware or engaged with others socially was practically a foreign concept.

———— ◆ ————

Crazy as it sounds, this is a big problem for many people. We think that joy is a natural state that anyone would be able to feel easily, given sufficient reason. And indeed, if you had a happy childhood and relatively trauma-free adulthood, you probably have a good size capacity for joy. Unfortunately, those circumstances are the exception rather than the rule.

The focus of my work with Patricia became mostly about increasing her capacity for connection to herself and to others. It included working through the awkwardness of it, of staying present when she wanted to withdraw, and feeling and processing unexpressed emotions from her past.

Gradually, she became more at home in her body. She began doing more things she enjoyed. She found herself liking her job more, stopping some unhealthy habits, and sleeping better. She had more energy. For years she had ruminated about where to take a vacation. Suddenly she made a firm choice about where she wanted to go and booked a trip. One day she declared, "I'm happy! I'm actually happy!"

Patricia continued to have challenges in her life, but she utilized her capacity for joy to help her cope with those challenges. And as she met each new challenge in a new way, her self-confidence and self-esteem grew.

What Gets in the Way

Too often, joy is attached to deserving. You believe you have to *do* something to earn it. It is a reward for your achievements, or for *being* good or *doing* good.

What messages do you give yourself when you fail to achieve a goal or behave in an ideal way? Over and over, I have witnessed people judging themselves harshly when things do not go the way they want. They blame themselves and punish themselves with self-criticism.

I have done it myself. For years I was a perfectionist and essentially in competition with an Ideal version of myself. I had such high expectations of myself that I could never live up to them. I believed I did not deserve to feel anything akin to joy. In fact, I would say self-judgment about not having achieved something I thought I *should* have not only caused me a lot of pain, it was my single biggest deterrent to success. Self-judgment caused me to disconnect from my true self. I could not see my value or my gifts because I had not *earned* them.

At the heart of all emotional pain is an experience of feeling profoundly alone and disconnected – cut off from your True Self, from others, from Spirit, God, Goddess, The Force, whatever you want to call It. And if you do not believe in a higher force, pain can be the result of feeling disconnected from your own values or sense of meaning.

Joy is possible for *everyone*, no matter how hard your life has been. No matter how much disappointment, trauma or pain you have suffered, joy is possible for you. Even more than possible it can be the very tool that will support and facilitate the healing and success that you deserve.

Blocks to Joy

The amount of joy you experience in life is greatly influenced by outside forces. You came into the world as a unique being, with an innate essence. Then the environments and circumstances you experienced growing up affected and shaped that essence, for better or worse, into the person you are now.

These influences fall into three main categories:

- The family or primary caregivers you grew up with

- Your ethnic culture

- The society in which you live(d)

Woven into all three areas are money and socio-economic status, gender and sexual orientation, and religion or spirituality, or lack thereof; your family of origin having the greatest impact. As you can see, it is complex.

All of this put together creates your conditioning. At the beginning of this manual, I said that each primary emotion has an inherent message that moves you away from pain and harm, or towards vitality and pleasure. Your conditioning is your habitual or predictable behavior that developed in order to avoid negative consequences.

Beliefs develop out of you trying to make sense of what is happening to you. At a young age, this can be completely unconscious.

Remember, our number one priority is survival. As a child, whenever you were hurt, did not feel safe, or did not feel validated, you did something to try and minimize the bad feeling and assure your safety. For example, some children withdraw into a fantasy world, while some act out to get the attention they need. The behavior can be blatant or subtle, like learning to never express anger or admitting that you are afraid.

At the same time, you develop beliefs in an attempt to make sense of your experience, beliefs like: I cannot trust anyone, I am unworthy, the world is not safe, or I am unlovable, to name a few.

Once a strategy works as a child, it quickly becomes a habitual choice. As adults, these habits may no longer serve us, but they have become so engrained we are unaware of them.

The beliefs you hold that dictate your choices can actually cause pain or harm, or at the very least, keep you stuck in a place you do not want to be in. These beliefs distort the natural instinct to move towards pleasure and away from pain, and you can end up doing the exact opposite, making choices that cause pain and keep you from fully enjoying life.

In order to create more joy in your life, you have to be willing to let go of old hurts and the stories that support them. Then you can make room for new stories and new feelings.

There was a reason for your difficulties, but you do not have to make it the definition of who you are. Too often we unconsciously live by the adage: *The devil I know is better than the devil I don't know*, so we stay attached to what we do not want for fear of the unknown.

Growing up I was taught that sacrifice was highly valued. Whenever I expressed wanting to do something that would be enjoyable, I was often told that I was selfish. So I learned to deny myself pleasure.

The most profound lesson I have learned is that I have the power to choose a different reality than the one I am experiencing. I discovered that the trick is not only to learn how to make new choices but to be willing to let go of the old ones.

Releasing Blocks to Joy

Albert Einstein famously described insanity as doing the same thing over and over again and expecting a different result. Habits are hard to break primarily because the motivation of those habits resides in your subconscious beliefs.

On top of that, beliefs are not just intangible concepts; they are physically embodied. Your beliefs and resulting habitual behavior create neuronal pathways in your brain, impact your nervous system, cause habitual muscle tension, and more.

The good news is that you can work with your body to support a new way of being. Something as simple as taking a deep breath when you become aware of tension in your body can have a profound impact on your state of mind. I recommend walking, yoga, the Chinese health practices of Tai Chi or Qigong, or *any* physical practice that creates energetic flow and balance in your body. It will support your mental and emotional growth process.

Let me give you a brief word of caution. Ironically, releasing blocks to joy can also bring up emotions you have repressed for a long time. Sometimes, it is enough to just stay present with these emotions and allow them to flow through you. Other times, writing in a journal or sharing them with a trusted friend or therapist can be highly beneficial.

Looking at Patterns

The goal here is to offer a key way to release conditioning that does not serve you. This is not a comprehensive look at all possible ways for all possible people. So, use this as a starting point.

Since we are often blind to our own habitual behavior, the easiest way to recognize where you could use a joy boost is to look at the patterns in your life. **Patterns reveal your conditioning and the underlying beliefs that support them**.

I will give you a real-life example of recognizing a pattern, determining the main emotions, and identifying the underlying belief.

———— •♦• ————

My client, Gayle, had been through a series of failed relationships over several years. I invited her to notice the common denominator in these relationships. The most obvious one to Gayle was herself. She was half of every relationship she was in. This may sound obvious at first, but so many people wrongly believe that they themselves do not contribute to their own unhappy circumstances.

She realized that no matter when she started seeing someone, they would break up just before Christmas or New Years.

This was both her favorite time of year and when she tended to feel most sentimental and vulnerable. She also recognized that she kept getting involved with men who were emotionally un-available, or had other issues that kept them at a distance.

Seeing these patterns, her "A-ha!" moment came when she rec-ognized that she was the one keeping men at a distance. Despite her desire to have a romantic relationship, she was actually terri-fied of intimacy. She was afraid to get close to someone because they would find out how flawed she was and she did not want anyone else to know it. What triggered this fear was a belief that something was fundamentally wrong with her. With this recogni-tion came feelings of shame, sadness and ultimately anger.

By recognizing her patterns and feeling the emotions that came up, Gayle was able to gain a new perspective on her herself. She acknowledged that it was pretty ridiculous that she thought of everyone else as being normal, while she was hopelessly flawed.

I helped her work on changing her belief and releasing her fears. She used her anger to fuel the actions she needed to take to fully release the belief. She decided that what was more important than a relationship was to work on herself, to build her sense of self-worth and self-confidence. I recently heard from Gayle and she is now happily married.

————•◆•————

The task then is to recognize the patterns that no longer serve you and then change any beliefs that hold them in place. In the next chapter I will outline two exercises for this purpose.

TWENTY-EIGHT

Exercises for Releasing Patterns and Beliefs

Exercise 1: Discovering Patterns and Beliefs

Start by looking at any patterns that exist in your life. You may be able to quickly identify a pattern by thinking about your history. Or, you may need to mull it over for awhile. To help you focus, here are four general categories to consider.

- **Romantic Relationships**
- **Friendships**
- **Job/Career/Business**
- **Health***

  *If you have serious health challenges and want to discover if there are underlying beliefs, I recommend working with a somatic therapist. In fact, having a skilled professional to help you through more engrained or serious issues of any kind can be very helpful. To find a therapist in your area, you can go to the US Association of Body Psychotherapy at usabp.org.

Once you have chosen a category, think about or make a list of any commonalities among people, circumstances or experiences. To help you further, answer the following questions:

1. What is a theme or pattern in this area?

2. What choices do you make that support this pattern?

3. What are common thoughts you have about your experiences in this area, and what emotions do you feel when you have these thoughts?

4. What must you believe to have these thoughts and feelings? Take your time here. You may need to do some journaling or stream of consciousness writing.

Once you have a belief to work with, do the Belief Change Guided Meditation that follows.

Exercise 2: Belief Change Meditation

Suggestion: If you do not have the audio version of this manual, you or someone else can record the following meditation for your use. You can also find an MP3 of this meditation on my website: <u>joieseldon.com/ emotionsmanual</u>.

To prepare for this meditation, write down the belief you have chosen to work with. Now, think of what belief you would like to have. You do not have to make it complicated. Simple is best. If your current belief is "I don't deserve to be happy," the new belief could be "I deserve to be happy." You get the idea.

Find a comfortable place to sit with your feet on the ground and back straight. Begin by becoming aware of your body. Notice your feet and legs and let them relax . . . relax your hands and arms . . . now, notice your neck and shoulders, let them relax . . . relax your chest . . . relax your stomach and belly . . . become aware of your breath. As you breathe, allow yourself to relax a little more, letting your breath flow down into your belly.

-   *Now, imagine before you, by seeing or simply sensing, a well-worn path that leads into the woods. Begin walking easily down the path. Notice that the path is going up a small hill, as it turns gently in one direction, now the other.*

- *As you come around a curve you see up ahead a clearing and a small hut. It looks inviting. As you walk forward, you know that in this is a special hut, where you will be changing a belief that no longer serves you. You reach the door and pause. Take a deep breath and exhale. Now open the door and step in.*

- *The light is dim. As your eyes adjust, you see the room is empty with another door on the opposite side. In just a few steps you reach the other door and open it. There you see stairs leading down. Step through to a small landing and the door behind you closes.*

- *Walk down the few stairs to reach the bottom where you notice a podium with a large book on top. Next to it is a simple stand with a gentle flame in the center of a disc. Step up to the book, which lays open. There you see your current belief written on the page. Set your intention to change this belief, to be done with it.*

- *Now, with great passion, rip the page out of the book. Enthusiastically tear the page in two, rip in up several times. Feel the power of releasing and destroying this old belief.*

- *Now turn to the flame. Put your torn page of the old belief into the flame and see it flare up. Watch it burn. See black wisps of burned paper float up then disintegrate. Feel the sense of relief. It is gone. It is over.*

- *Now go back to the book and see that there is a blank page showing, and a pen next to it. With great passion, write in your new belief. See it on the page. Feel the emotion of what this new belief means. Feel the joy that it will bring you. Now close the book, knowing you have created something that will support you moving forward.*

- *Turn and walk up the stairs, through the hut, and out the front door. The daylight may be a bit bright at first. As your eyes adjust, see how beautiful everything is, the blue sky, the white clouds, the greenery around you. Walk back down the path feeling the joy of your new life.*

- *Now, allow yourself to become aware of your body, being in the room you are in, sensing your surroundings as you gently open your eyes.*

To support the integration of your new belief, write it on a post-it or 3x5 card, something you can put where you can see it, and feel it, on a daily basis.

TWENTY-NINE

Making New Choices

You are a choice-making machine. And, there is a direct correlation between your emotions and the choices you make. Of the dozens if not hundreds of choices you make every day, most are automatic. Many are fairly inconsequential, like eating cereal for breakfast. Others have a substantial impact.

Marie always finds an excuse for not attending the networking events that will help her business. Whenever Scott meets a woman he is attracted to, he overwhelms her with too much attention. Grace calls her grown daughter every day and wonders why she won't come home for a visit. These are emotion driven choices.

In order to experience more joy in your life, it is good to bring more awareness to the choices you make. Here is a simple tool to help you make more conscious choices.

Is it a Fear Choice or a Growth Choice?

To discover what is motivating the choices you make, ask yourself: "Is this choice motivated by fear? Or, will this choice help me grow?"

When Marie decides to stay home and watch her favorite TV show instead of going to a networking event, she asks herself, "Is this a fear choice, or a growth choice?" The answer is so obvious it makes her laugh. She decides to go to the networking event and gives herself permission to leave if it is really unbearable.

When Scott feels the impulse at nine o'clock in the morning to call the woman he had a first date with the night before, he asks himself, "Is this a fear choice or a growth choice?" At first, he is confused. He doesn't think it is either one. Then, he realizes that he is terrified of ending up alone in life and that the people he dates must sense his desperation.

Any habit that you have that you wonder about, ask yourself, "Do I do this out of fear? Or because it makes me grow?" This tool is especially helpful when you are unsure about what to do. If the answer is unclear, put your hands over your solar plexus, this is the space above your belly button and below your breastbone, and ask, "Is this (fill in the blank) in my best interest?" If you feel your solar plexus contracting or closing, it is a fear choice. If it opens up or you feel lighter, it is a growth choice. This is your body's wisdom communicating with you.

This technique can be used for things like, "should I eat this cookie?" to major life decisions. If you get no response from your body, it is most likely something that is not bad for you, but not especially beneficial. It is neutral, so your body is neutral. If you are not used to tuning into your body in this way, it may take a few times before the message is clear. What is important is to follow what you get and take action.

Cultivating Joy

The definition of cultivate is "to prepare and use soil for growing plants: to grow or raise something under conditions that you can control."

What I love about this definition are the words *under conditions that you can control*. An important aspect of Emotional Intelligence is your ability to be in charge of your emotions without suppressing or denying them or allowing them to be in charge of you.

The first step in cultivation is to prepare the soil, which is what we have been doing so far in this segment on joy. Breaking up the hard-packed ground of disempowering habits born out of your conditioning, removing rocks of old beliefs, turning over the soil of your awareness to bring in more light and oxygen, allowing for a greater understanding of who you have been and who you want to be.

You are now ready to plant some seeds and fertilize them.

Planting Seeds

You plant the seeds by setting your intentions. What will bring you more joy? Your intention is how you focus your energy and actions on creating what you want. Your intention may be to be done with your pain, to create greater professional successful, or have more financial abundance. It might be to have the relationship you have longed for or to improve the relationships you have, or simply to live a more fulfilling and enjoyable life.

If all you know is, "I don't what I have now!" that is OK. It is how I got started on my path. Once I was clear about what I did not want, I discovered that my greatest desires became to know what was the truth about life and what was my purpose. At the time I set those intentions, I did not know, nor could I have predicted, my life now. Yet, the feelings I have now are exactly what I wanted to feel back then – alive, engaged in life, and more joyful than I have even been.

I invite you to take a moment now to think about what it is that you really want. What is it you long for from your soul? What would bring you joy? What seed do you want to plant? Write down what comes up for you.

It is important to say out loud what you want. Otherwise, your psyche thinks it is a secret, and how can it be supported if no one knows? You need to declare it, and then claim it as your right.

I invite you to do this now. Say out loud what you want starting with the words, "I want ___ (your desire) ___." Then, stake your claim by saying out loud, "I claim my right to have ___ (your desire)___!"

You may then want to create or find something that represents what you want. It can be a symbol you create that you can put on a 3x5 card. Or a physical representation, such as an icon, a statue or a vision board placed where you can see it as a reminder. Get creative with it.

Once you have planted the seed of your intention, you need to water it and give it some fertilizer. This can be done in the form of reading inspirational books, taking a class or workshop that supports your intention, getting bodywork or exercising. In other words, taking some kind of positive action.

You may also need to pull some weeds. Habits of belief are like weeds, and habitual behavior seldom dies off easily. You may have to pull the same weed out many times. Keep pulling. You may want to review certain sections of this manual or go back to some of the exercises.

It is always helpful to have some kind of personal support, a therapist, a life or business coach, or a support group or mastermind group, for example. Another option is to have an accountability partner. Connecting with others for mutual support is invaluable. I have been in a mastermind group for some time with two people I met professionally.

This last segment is all about watering, fertilizing and growing your garden of joy. It requires commitment and patience, but once you see the first signs of growth it gets easier and easier.

In this segment we are going to cover some essential components for tending your garden of joy, including three key areas where you can create a greater sense of connection, and some simple actions you can take to evoke joy. I will conclude with teaching you the Emotional Fluidity Exercise, a profound technique that conditions you for more joy.

In support of your journey, you may want to start a *joy journal*, or create an alter or a vision board that represents your 'garden of joy.'

Three Keys To Create More Connection In Your Life

Remember, Joy is the emotion of connection. So the following three keys have to do with connecting with yourself, connecting with others, and connecting with something greater than yourself.

Key #1: You Connecting With YOU

At the heart of cultivating joy is self-acceptance. Are you hard on yourself? Are you a perfectionist? Do have expectations of yourself that you have not met, and judge yourself for? Do you have an inner critic that constantly demands more of you?

All of these things can keep you from connecting with yourself. Connecting with yourself is about loving yourself. Self-love can be challenging, for sure, but it is not about loving yourself perfectly. It is about recognizing when you are judging yourself and declaring, "I don't want to do that to myself." Then forgive yourself and move on. For me, this is a life-long practice.

The thing is, we all want to be seen and heard by others, but too often we do not take the time to see and hear our self. Here are three keys to seeing, hearing, and connecting with yourself.

1. **Unconditional Acceptance**: You are probably harder on yourself than anyone else. You are not perfect. Most likely you have made bad choices, done stupid things, and hurt people. This comes with the territory of being human. It is not that you should take your misdeeds too lightly, but too often we err on the side of self-punishment, rather than self-acceptance.

    My husband is very good at recognizing his missteps, feeling embarrassment, shame or sadness as is appropriate, then moving on. He is willing to forgive himself, and he is not arrogance about it. I was not used to this. In the beginning, it annoyed me that he did not suffer as I did. After a few years of this, I decided his way was much better.

    I invite you to make a commitment to totally accept everything you do without judgment for three days. Feel whatever emotions come, but do not use the situation to punish yourself. I know this can be difficult for many people. It is hard to let yourself off the hook, and sometimes to let other off as well. Do your best.

2. **Cultivate Intimacy with Yourself**: Intimacy starts with emotional honesty. Tell yourself the truth emotionally. Acknowledge your sadness, your fear, or anger. Be present with your insecurities.

Also, be present with your gifts. Acknowledge all the positive things about yourself that you have been afraid to admit for fear of being seen as egotistical. What are you good at? What skills do you have? What comes naturally to you? What do you care about?

Here are two options for creating more intimacy with yourself:

- The first is to set a timer for fifteen minutes and sit in front of a mirror. Look yourself in the eye. Look at the person before you. Tell that person in the mirror what you like about him or her. Dig as deep as you can to acknowledge everything, big and small, that you like or admire about you. If emotions come up in this exercise, simply be with them.

- The second is to write a one-page love letter to yourself every day for seven days. Write things you appreciate about yourself, your qualities and kindnesses. If seven days sound intimidating to you, trust that you will find things to write about.

3. **Choose You, Choose Joy**: You are you. You will never be anyone else. Make the most of it! Stop comparing yourself to others. Commit yourself to be the best 'You' you can be. Enjoy yourself! The ability to *choose* to feel joy can be a source of tremendous personal power because it moves you into alignment with your Self with a capital S. Choice is one of the most powerful tools that we have.

I suggest creating a self-affirming affirmation. One of my issues in the past was that I never felt like I really belonged anywhere. I felt out of place. I came up with a simple affirmation, *"I belong here."* Anytime I felt myself out of place, or not belonging, in my mind I would think, "I belong here." This became my mantra. What would be a mantra that supports you?

Key #2: Connect With Others

You can have different levels of connection with other people. Some are superficial, some friendly but not deep, and some are close and trusted friends, and then there is that rare person who you can be totally honest with, revealing your deepest thoughts and feelings and connecting in a profound way.

If you are someone who does not have anyone like this in your life, I highly recommend seeking a spiritual or therapeutic counselor as a stepping stone to drawing into your life a close friend or partner. A major turning point in my life was the first time I went into therapy.

Learning how to really connect with others has been the hardest part of my personal growth. My childhood conditioning resulted in my being a kind of a loner. I was independent and self-sufficient, and this served me well in many ways in my young adulthood. But, I was also lonely for a long time. It was not until I was forty-two that I was able to enter into a long-term relationship.

Quick Word to Those of You in a Committed Relationship

When there is tension, an argument, or stuff you are grappling with that you are reluctant to share with your partner, it is common to want to turn away from him or her. And, sometimes we do need time and space to process our experience on our own. That said, I strongly advise turning *toward* your partner when you are unhappy.

My relationship with my husband has grown and flourished because we have learned, over time, to stay connected when we are unhappy with each other. It can be frustrating, awkward, uncomfortable, but so rewarding to stay connected with each other during discord. Like every couple, we get into situations where we are trying to prove "I'm right and you're wrong." But, by staying present with each other and taking the time to keep communicating until we really understand the other one's point of view and feelings, we not only come to an understanding, our trust, love, and affection for each other grows. Staying connected through discord builds trust, and a sincere apology can create greater intimacy.

Creating More Connection

Take some time now to think about what kind of relationships you have. Do they produce joy or not? How would you like to be in your relationships? Is there a friend, partner, or loved one who you would like to feel closer to? What step can you take to create a greater connection with that person?

Here are some suggestions:

- Reach out to that person with the intention of connecting with them on a deeper level. You can use this manual as your reason. Tell them, *"I'm working on creating more joy in my life and I have an assignment to do and I thought of you. I'd like to get to know you better."*

- If it is your significant other, you can say something similar, for example, *"I feel like we could have more joy in our relationship."* Word it in any way that feels right to you. If you feel awkward or nervous, acknowledge it. Say, *"I feel kind of awkward talking about this, but . . . "* You might be surprised at how open someone would be to this, and they may feel really honored. Instead of only talking about problems in your relationships, talk about how you can create more joy!

- Be willing to be vulnerable. Honesty about your own insecurities can make others feel more open and at ease. It may feel risky, but the gain far out ways the possible awkwardness.

Key #3: Connect to Something Greater Than You

The final key is about connecting to something greater than you. Whether you call it God, Spirit, nature or simply The Universe, having a sense of connection with something greater than yourself can help you to feel like you are not alone. That *something* is there to support you in your journey to wholeness.

No single religion or belief system works for everyone. It is important to discover what gives you the greatest sense of joy in your life. If that means you do not believe in something greater than yourself, I support you.

In my quest to find what the truth is about life, I discovered spiritual tenets that work for me. My sense of connection to something greater than myself has been an important part of my journey.

———— ◆ ————

Finally, beneath all of your "stuff," your pain, your disempowering beliefs, and conditioning, you are innately connected to life itself. What brings this into focus quicker than anything I know is gratitude. I am hardly the first to tout this. Many people teach the benefit of gratitude. It is a big "YES" to life and a puts your whole being into a vibration of abundance. I recommend it.

THIRTY

Evoking Joy

As you may have discerned by now, joy is a bit different than the other foundational emotions. With all emotions, it is beneficial to increase your ability to feel them and let them flow through you. However, I would not suggest you intentionally do activities in your life that evoke sadness, fear or anger. With joy, however, it can be beneficial to do things that will evoke the emotion of joy so you can "practice" feeling it.

Ironically, you may actually feel uncomfortable experiencing new-found joy. Sounds crazy, right? But for some people, feeling good is not as easy as it sounds. This was my experience. I was used to feeling sad and lonely and believed that I had not earned the right to feel joy. Sadness was comfortable; joy, not so much.

When I began experiencing more joy, I was not used to so much energy flowing through my body. In a way, my nervous system had to recalibrate itself. Sometimes I literally had to move around or shake my body to keep from resisting the sensation of joy.

Too many people sit on their joy; they do not allow themselves to really feel it. Is that you? Shifting into a state of joy takes courage, but it also takes practice. I invite you to simply give it a try.

Two Essentials for Cultivating Joy

First: Proactive Engagement

The first essential is to engage in activities that make you feel good and that help you experience connection. Do not wait for something to happen that makes you feel joy.

You can intentionally shift from the state you are into a state of joy. When you find yourself stressed, anxious, checked out, getting angry over small things, or any other state that is part of an unhappy norm, there are some quick and easy things you can do that can help you move into a joyful state. Even if you do not experience a clear sense of joy in doing these activities, you are sending yourself the message that you are in charge of your emotions.

On the surface, these may seem almost too simple. But do not let their simplicity deceive you. They are powerful tools.

Here are some ways to practice joy:

- Think of something you are grateful for. Gratitude is one of the greatest antidotes to misery.

- Listen to music that makes you feel good.

- Move your body. Dance around or stand up and shake for a few minutes, three to five minutes is a good length. If you love to dance, make a commitment to go dancing at a club or join a class.

- Look at something that makes you feel good: a photo of someone you love, a spiritual teacher, a beautiful view. For example, every January I invest in a beautiful wall calendar for my office.

- Go for a walk, even if it is just around the block.

- Exercise in a way you enjoy. It's a great preventative measure and will raise your overall capacity for joy.

- Connect to nature, even if it is just stepping into your backyard or going to a local park.

- Spend time with your pet if you have one.

- Watch a funny TV show or movie. I have certain feel good movies I turn to.

- Call a friend, not to complain, but to connect with someone you like. You can even say, "Hey, I'm working on connecting more with people, and I thought of you. How are you?"

- Something many people struggle with is isolation. Finding some kind of community with people of like mind or like interests promotes joy.

- Do something for someone else. You might want to volunteer for an organization or non-profit.

You get the idea. You can do any or all of these things, or come up with your own activities. What is important is to develop a habit of turning towards joy and connection.

Second: Develop Emotional Fluidity

This entire manual has been about helping you to clear out old, unprocessed, unexpressed emotions, *and* to develop the skills to experience, understand and value your feelings in beneficial ways.

Emotional Fluidity is when you can stay present with whatever emotion you are feeling, preferably without judgment, and listen to its message. Then, if called for, take appropriate action, which may or may not include expressing that feeling outwardly. As you gain Emotional Intelligence, this seemingly lengthy process becomes more instinctual, and it can happen in a matter of seconds.

For the most part, children do this naturally; they can be playing one minute, crying the next, and laughing the next. Unfortunately, this fluidity gets conditioned out of us. When you are *emotionally fluid*, emotions will move more freely through your body and being. Some of the benefits are that you can move on from upsets more easily, recognize your own imperfections without excessive self-judgment, and communicate with other with greater clarity.

What follows is the most powerful exercise I know of for practicing and developing *emotional fluidity*. One way to think of this exercise is as a kind of emotion yoga. It is meant to create energetic flow and vitality as well as tone your emotional muscles. It is a way to say to your body, "It's OK to feel these emotions," so that you become more accepting of the sensations and visceral experience of them. Equally important, it is OK to let them go. It is also a great tool for getting unstuck or gaining clarity about a particular issue or situation.

The Emotional Fluidity Exercise entails moving through the four emotions in a particular order, which will help you experience the organic relationship between these cornerstone emotions. There is an energetic flow when you express them in this order. And best of all, you always end in joy!

To begin, here is a quick review the four emotions:

SADNESS: Sadness is about loss or perceived loss. In sadness, your focus turns inward and your body functions slow down. You can sense it as an *inward moving energy* with a slow vibration.

FEAR: Fear is a warning of possible danger, real or projected, tangible or intangible. Unless your life is directly threatened, fear's message is "Stop, pay attention! Be conscious." Your body contracts when you feel fear, so it is also an *inward moving energy*. However, it is a faster vibration than sadness.

ANGER: Anger occurs when there is a threat to your body, your autonomy, or your values. It sets boundaries. "No! I don't like this/want this!" As a boundary setter, it is *an outward moving energy* that is directed at someone or something (rather than away from it as in fear) resulting in an often more intense vibration than fear.

JOY: Joy is the emotion of connection – to yourself, or something or someone outside yourself. It is a sense of oneness or non-separation. It is an *outward moving energy* that is omnidirectional. Whether joy is experienced as excitement or deep peace, its vibration is very high.

THIRTY-ONE

Becoming Emotionally Fluid — The Exercise

I have saved the best for last. If you do nothing else going forward, do this exercise. It brings together so much of what we have covered in a deceptively simple practice that takes only a few minutes to do.

It is a light-hearted way to get used to letting your emotion come and go. So, you do not have to fear being overwhelmed by an emotion, or feel that you have to control your feelings.

This exercise has two overall objectives. The first is to wake up your emotional body, in essence to give yourself permission to experience and express your feelings. This includes connecting your emotions and their meaning with specific body sensations so you can be more aware of what you are feeling when you are feeling it. The second purpose is to use it as a tool for getting unstuck.

Throughout this book, I have talked about specific ways we experience different emotions in our body. In both versions of this exercise, the basic task is to engage your body in a way that you act as if you are feeling each of the four foundation emotions. This means engaging your whole body and voice.

If you have ever seen children playing at make-believe you know they have no problem pretending to have strong emotions. You still have that innate ability to make-believe. This is really about pretending or acting-as-if you are feeling various emotions in an exaggerated way. You may feel awkward or silly and that is OK. Do not let that stop you from doing it full out. I cannot emphasize enough the profound benefits of this simple exercise.

Although the goal is not to feel a genuine emotion, you may very well have that experience. That is fine. Do not resist it, but don't feel that you have to make that happen. You will want to do this in a private place, where you can fully express yourself.

I will lay out the process of expressing each of the four emotions by describing what to do with your body and the words to say. As I go through each emotion, let your body follow and respond to my description. Always express the emotions in the same order of sadness, fear, anger and joy.

While I recommend reading through the exercise first, it may be easiest to understand by watching a demonstration. There are videos on my website where I demonstrate both versions of the exercise. Go to www.joieseldon.com/EFE.

Emotional Flow

Before we begin, notice how your body feels right now. Notice any tension or numbness or other sensations. Make note of that. Be present.

SADNESS

- Let your body go slack, letting go of any muscle tension. Let your head drop down and curve your shoulders forward. Sense your chest caving in. Take on a sad expression on your face and say with a sad voice, *"I'm sad. I am so sad. I've lost something I really value. I'm so sad."* Sigh. *"I'm sad."* Take your time with it.

Move into fear.

FEAR

- Stand or sit up straighter, and bend your elbows, bringing your hands up in front of your chest in tight fists. Tighten the muscles in your arms and chest. At the same time, pull your head back while keeping your chin down, as if you want to move away from something threatening. Inhale and hold your breath for a second then breathe shallowly. Let your eyes get wide, and say, *"I'm afraid. I'm really scared. Stop! I don't want to be hurt! I'm so scared. I'm afraid."*

Move into anger.

ANGER

- Your body is still tense, but stand or sit up straighter. Keeping your hands in fists, and let your arms straighten mostly, but not all the way. Tighten your upper arms. Take on an expression of anger, pushing your eyebrows down. As you speak thrust your fists down and up again repeatedly as if you are hammering and say with energy saying, *"I'm angry! I'm angry! I don't like this!*

I'm angry! I'm so angry." Now open your hands and thrust your palms forward and say, *"No! I don't want this! No! This is not OK with me. I'm angry."*

Move into joy.

JOY

- Relax your face and body, standing up straight, open your chest, open your arms wide. Smile. Take a deep breath and exhale, and say *"Yes! I feel joy! Yay! I feel joy. I feel connected. I feel open and free. Yes. I feel joy! YES! "*

Now let it all go. Shake it loose. Take a breath and exhale. Notice how you feel.

Try doing this again on your own, or with the demo on the website. As you switch to the next emotion, change your body posture and demeanor as I just instructed. Remember to exaggerate your movements and vocal expression. You do not have to say exactly what I say. You can copy me, or say any words that express the emotion. Have fun with it.

When you are done with the exercise, notice how you feel. Do you feel different than before you did the exercise? If so, in what way? What is different? Perhaps you feel more energy in your body.

Getting Unstuck

Whenever you procrastinate or otherwise feel stuck in some area of your life, there is always an emotion that is not being processed, whether you are aware of it or not.

Think of an area of your life where you feel stuck, confused or unsure. It can be tangible, or intangible. For example: *I can't decide whether to take this class or not. I hate my job, but I can't seem to do anything about it. I don't know what I want.*

To start with, you might want to pick something you are

procrastinating about. It does not have to be anything large. It can be simple like not mowing the lawn. Take a moment to think of what you want to work with.

Similar to the version we just did, you will act out the four emotions. Use your body and tone of voice to express each emotion in the same exaggerated way. Only this time, talk out loud about your issue and express the emotion in relation to your issue.

While it is OK if you do not feel a genuine emotion, what most likely will happen is that one or more emotions will feel real, or at least more real than the others. The point of using the Emotional Fluidity Exercise is to free up stuck emotions, the ones you have not acknowledge or have not processed. Again, you can go to the website for a demonstration.

Let us assume that I've been procrastinating about exercising. It would sound something like this:

"I am so sad that I don't exercise. I'm so sad. I know I need to exercise. I know I feel better when I do, but I just feel so sad about it. It's a lot harder now than when I was younger. I'm sad to lose my youthful tone and energy. It just makes me feel sad." (Shift into fear.)

"I'm scared to exercise. It's too scary. What if I get hurt? What if I keep exercising and my body doesn't change? And I get weaker instead of stronger. I'm scared of how much work it would be now." (Shift into anger.)

I'm so angry that I don't exercise! I don't want to exercise. It's too hard! I know I need to and I'm angry with myself for not being disciplined enough to do it. But, it's boring. I hate exercising! I'm so angry about it. (Shift into joy.)

I love to exercise! I feel so good when I exercise. I feel powerful. It's joyful to move my body. I love feeling my body getting stronger and stronger! I feel great!

You may have noticed that when I got to joy, I expressed what I would feel doing what I was resisting. For joy, express what it would be like to have your issue resolved and you get to experience what you want. It could simply be how good it feels to have gotten a task done, or it could have to do with the direct benefit of the action you take, whatever that is.

If you have not thought of something already, think of an area where you feel stuck. Try doing the sequence of emotions on your own, or go to the website and do it along with me there. Of course, I won't know what you have chosen to work with, so my words will be about the emotion. It is up to you to speak specifically about your issue. And, do it out loud! There is something about hearing your own voice expressing yourself that is very empowering. It gets you past lines of resistance.

There are two things to keep in mind. One is to be big, exaggerating the emotions, letting yourself be over the top or absurd. It keeps you from being too precious, or serious. It also wakes up your subconscious mind. Second, don't try to figure out the right things to say. Open your mouth and just start talking aloud. There are no "right words."

If you have done the exercise, did you notice if one of the emotions felt more genuine than the others? If so, that's the emotion that is keeping you stuck. If one emotion stood out, spend some time tuning into that particular emotion around this issue. Be curious about it and let yourself feel it.

If none of them felt real, it may mean that you need to work with the first version for a while to wake up your emotional body. I advise doing the Emotional Fluidity Exercise every day for 7 days. If you are willing to commit, do 21 days in a row. It can take you as little as 2 minutes to go through the four emotions. Of course, you can take longer, but even a quick run through has benefits.

Once you begin to experience the benefits, you can do it on your own in a variety of ways. You can go big, or you can sit quietly going through the emotions as a kind of meditation. If you are an artistic person, try painting it, singing it, improvising with an instrument, or just makes sounds, or move your body in a kind of emotion dance. Do come back to using words, though.

THIRTY-TWO

The Road to Emotional Mastery

Over the course of this manual we have covered a lot of material. Let's briefly review the key components. Since you now have a different perspective of the material than when you started, as you read the following I invite you to notice how the information strikes you now. Does it have a new meaning for you? Does it make more sense?

———— ◆ ————

- Emotions are a body-based information system the purpose of which is to prompt you to action that is optimally beneficial for your survival and wellbeing.

- There are four primary emotions that provide a foundation for all other feelings. Beyond the purpose of pure survival, these emotions and their modern-day messages are:

  » Fear, which wants you to pay attention.

  » Anger, which says no, this is not OK with me.

  » Sadness, which wants you to honor and process your losses, tangible and intangible.

  » Joy, which is about experiencing connection and belonging.

- All emotions are inherently positive (constructive). It is repression, denial or the misinterpretation of them that turns them into something negative (destructive).

- When you acknowledge your emotions and listen to their

message, you have the power to make conscious choices and direct your life in a purposeful manner.

- Your emotions are not meant to run the show. You are meant to be the one in charge. They are a resource for you to know yourself, and to support you in creating the life you want to live.

- It is possible to learn how to manage your emotions, which empowers you to be more fully who you are. Having dominion of your emotions positively impacts your professional and personal relationships. It also reduces stress and benefits your health.

———————◆———————

I have a question for you. What do you see as possible for you now that you did not see before reading this manual?

The process of becoming emotionally intelligent is a journey more than a destination. It is not a place to which you arrive. It is a tool to navigate life in a way that is fulfilling for you. It is an ongoing process that deepens over time.

The path is not a straight line. It is circuitous and spiraling. You may revisit old habits and automatic responses many times on your way to change. It can be challenging and even difficult work to change your way of being.

However, your ability to make better choices for yourself will steadily increase as you become more and more emotionally present in your life. Being present with your emotions is where you have the power to choose a new interpretation of what your emotions mean. That is what allows you to choose a new behavior. It takes courage to be in charge of your experience. And, as with many things that take courage, the payoff is high.

———————◆———————

I will end with a story about a client I will call Jane. Jane is an executive in an international company. After surviving a life-threatening disease, she returned to work, but something was different. Her sense of self-confidence was gone. She worried all the time about how she was doing, and what others thought of her, especially her boss. She also had to deal with some very difficult family issues and was in a constant state of stress.

As we worked together over time, she built her ability to recognize the specific emotions she had, up to that point, been calling "stress." She was able to see how her worrisome thinking diminished her ability to function. She learned how to become more of a witness to her emotions, which allowed her to access her knowledge and be more purposeful at her job.

She also learned to handle her family situation by setting healthy boundaries. As she practiced the skills of emotional management and clear communication with others, her confidence grew. She was able to improve her relationship with someone whom she had often been upset with. She started enjoying her life more and worrying less. Recently, at the end our session she said, "I'm no longer afraid."

———— ◆ ————

A kind of phenomenon I have witnessed over the years is that when someone takes charge of their own emotions, understands their own responses, and becomes proactive in their relationships, the world around them changes. The coworker who drove them crazy quits or is transferred. The friend or family member who was a source of pain changes their behavior. The boss who seemed to be their nemesis becomes their advocate.

Whatever the issues or challenges of your life are, they can be improved by increasing your emotional intelligence – your ability to be aware of your emotions, to name them, to understand their meaning, and then to use this knowledge to act accordingly. Not only will this result in greater fulfillment in your life, it has a positive impact on those you come in contact with.

I invite you to use this manual as a launching pad and an ongoing resource to empower yourself in your journey to a more fulfilling life.

———————•◆•———————

Personal Message From Joie:

While developing my Emotional Intelligence has had professional rewards, what I am most grateful for is the quality of my relationships, especially with my husband. Also, my relationship with myself, how I feel about myself, has improved dramatically.

I used to be a very sad person and tried so hard to put on a good face to cover up my doubt and pain. I had an idea of who I wanted to be but had no idea how to be that person. Being willing to feel my emotions has been the key to so much of what is good in my life now.

More than anything, I wish for you curiosity and willingness to un-cover your truest self, and the courage to walk your path. The world needs you. You matter. What you experience inside yourself matters.

Care for yourself. It is not selfish to do that. It is the single best thing you can do for others, and for this crazy planet that we live on.

Being emotionally connected is your birthright. Turn towards your emotions, not away from them. Wake up to the richness of your emo-tional self.

We humans are an ever-evolving species. So much emphasis has been on doing and achieving, or on just surviving. It is time to focus on a new frontier, that of the human *being*. Take a moment right now to acknowledge the miracle and the mystery of who you are.

I do not believe anything happens by accident or happenstance. We are all here for a purpose. What's yours?

Bibliography

Bradberry, Travis and Greaves, Jean. Emotional Intelligence 2.0. San Diego: Talent Smart, 2009.

Bradshaw, John. Healing the Shame That Binds Me. Florida: Health Communications, Inc., 1988.

Damasio, Anthony. The Feeling Of What Happens: Body And Emotions In The Making Of Consciousness. San Diego: A Harvest Book, Harcourt, Inc., 1999.

Damasio, A Looking for Spinoza, Joy Sorrow, and the Feeling Brain. Orlando: Harcourt, Inc., 2003.

Darwin, C. The Expression of The Emotions In Man and Animals. Chicago: The University of Chicago Press, 1965/1872.

DeBecker, Gavin. The Gift of Fear. Canada: Little, Brown & Company, Ltd, 1997.

Dello Joio, Vicki. The Way of Joy. Oregon: Wyatt-MacKenzie Publishing, 2009.

Dozier, Jr., R.W. Fear Itself. New York: St. Martin's Press, 1998.

Dunham, Robert and Denning, Peter. The Innovator's Way: Essential Practices for Successful Innovation. MIT Press, 2012.

Ekman, Paul. Emotions Revealed. New York: Henry Hold and Company, 2003.

Ellison, Sharon. Taking The War Out of Our Words. Berkeley: Bay Tree, 1998.

Fosha, D. The Transforming Power Of Affect. New York: Basic Books, 2000.

Goleman, Daniel. Emotional Intelligence. New York: Bantam, 1995.

Gray, John, Ph.D. Venus on Fire Mars on Ice. British Columbia, Canada: Mind Publishing, 2010.

Hicks, Esther and Jerry. The Astonishing Power of Emotions. California: Hay House, 2007.

Johnston, V. Why We Feel, The Science of Human Emotions. Reading, MA: Perseus Books, 1999.

Keleman, S. Emotional Anatomy. California: Center Press, 1989.

Kinder, M. Mastering Your Moods. New York: Simon & Schuster, 1994.

LeDoux, Joseph. The Emotional Brain. New York: Simon & Schuster, 1996.

Masters, Augustus. "Compassionate Wrath: Transpersonal Approaches to Anger." https://www.atpweb.org/pdf/masters.pdf. 2000.

McLaren, Karla. Emotional Genius. California: Laughing Tree Press, 2001.

Nelson, Bradley. The Emotion Code. Nevada: Wellness Unmasked Publishing, 2007.

Pert, C. Molecules of Emotions. New York: Scribner, 1997.

Porges, Steven. "Emotions: An Evolutionary By-Product of the Neural Regulation of The Autonomic Nervous System." New York Academy of Sciences, 1997. http://onlinelibrary.wiley.com/doi/10.1111/j.1749-6632.1997.tb51913.x/abstract

Siegel, D. The Developing Mind. New York: The Guilford Press, 1999.

Printed in the USA
CPSIA information can be obtained
at www.ICGtesting.com
LVHW022359150923
758231LV00009B/351

9 781478 787280